EQUAL JUSTICE UNDER LAW

THE SUPREME COURT IN AMERICAN LIFE

By MARY ANN HARRELL
National Geographic Staff
and BURNETT ANDERSON

THE SUPREME COURT HISTORICAL SOCIETY

with the cooperation of the National Geographic Society

WASHINGTON, D. C.

*Produced as a public service
by the National Geographic Society*

Gilbert M. Grosvenor	President and Chairman of the Board
Melvin M. Payne	Chairman Emeritus
Thomas W. McKnew	Chairman Emeritus
Owen R. Anderson	Executive Vice President
Robert L. Breeden	Senior Vice President, Publications and Educational Media

Prepared by the Special Publications Division

Donald J. Crump	Director
Philip B. Silcott	Associate Director
Bonnie S. Lawrence	Assistant Director

STAFF FOR FIRST EDITION: Jules B. Billard, Bruce Brander, Abigail T. Brett, Thomas Canby, Jr., Dorothy Corson, Barbara Coulter, Richard M. Crum, Johanna G. Farren, Barbara J. Hall, Carolyn Hatt, Geraldine Linder, Margaret C. Shaw, O. Mac White, Peggy D. Winston

STAFF FOR THIS EDITION: Elizabeth W. Fisher, Editor; Charles M. Kogod, Picture Editor; Corinne Szabo, Designer; Alice K. Jablonsky, Researcher; Jolene M. Blozis, Indexer; Rosamund Garner, Editorial Assistant; Susan A. Bender, Sharon K. Berry, Mary Elizabeth Ellison, Kaylene Kahler, Sandra F. Lotterman, Eliza C. Morton, Staff Assistants

ENGRAVING, PRINTING, AND PRODUCT MANUFACTURE: Robert W. Messer, Manager; David V. Showers, Production Manager; Kevin P. Heubusch, Production Project Manager

Fifth Edition, 1988
Library of Congress Catalog Card Number 88-061126; ISBN 0-914785-03-6

SOLITARY STAR *below the American eagle distinguishes the Seal of the Supreme Court of the United States. Justices ordered the emblem at their third meeting, on February 3, 1790. Its designers adapted the Great Seal of the United States, adding the star to symbolize the Constitution's grant of judicial power to "one Supreme Court." The Clerk of the Court affixes the Seal to official papers —judgments, mandates, and writs.*

CONTENTS

EQUAL JUSTICE UNDER LAW

The Supreme Court in American Life

Revised Edition

THE SUPREME COURT HISTORICAL SOCIETY

JAMES WILSON
1789-98

JOHN JAY*
1789-95

WILLIAM CUSHING
1790-1810

JOHN BLAIR
1790-96

SAMUEL CHASE
1796-1811

OLIVER ELLSWORTH*
1796-1800

BUSHROD WASHINGTON
1799-1829

ALFRED MOORE
1800-04

JOHN MARSHALL*
1801-35

SMITH THOMPSON
1823-43

ROBERT TRIMBLE
1826-28

JOHN McLEAN
1830-61

HENRY BALDWIN
1830-44

JOHN McKINLEY
1838-52

PETER VIVIAN DANIEL
1842-60

SAMUEL NELSON
1845-72

LEVI WOODBURY
1845-51

ROBERT C. GRIER
1846-70

DAVID DAVIS
1862-77

STEPHEN J. FIELD
1863-97

SALMON P. CHASE*
1864-73

WILLIAM STRONG
1870-80

WILLIAM B. WOODS
1881-87

STANLEY MATTHEWS
1881-89

HORACE GRAY
1882-1902

ENDPAPERS: *One hundred and four Justices have served on the Supreme Court since its beginnings in 1789. The rows of portraits running horizontally across both pages present the jurists, with terms of service, in order of taking the oath*

JOHN RUTLEDGE*
1790-91; 1795

JAMES IREDELL
1790-99

THOMAS JOHNSON
1792-93

WILLIAM PATERSON*
1793-1806

WILLIAM JOHNSON
1804-34

HENRY B. LIVINGSTON
1807-23

THOMAS TODD
1807-26

GABRIEL DUVALL
1811-35

JOSEPH STORY
1812-45

JAMES MOORE WAYNE
1835-67

ROGER B. TANEY*
1836-64

PHILIP P. BARBOUR
1836-41

JOHN CATRON
1837-65

BENJAMIN R. CURTIS
1851-57

JOHN A. CAMPBELL
1853-61

NATHAN CLIFFORD
1858-81

NOAH HAYNES SWAYNE
1862-81

SAMUEL F. MILLER
1862-90

JOSEPH P. BRADLEY
1870-92

WARD HUNT
1873-82

MORRISON R. WAITE*
1874-88

JOHN M. HARLAN
1877-1911

Asterisks indicate the 16 judges who have served as Chief Justice.

OVERLEAF: *James Earle Fraser's "Contemplation of Justice" sits brooding before the main entrance of the Supreme Court.*

SAMUEL BLATCHFORD
1882-93

LUCIUS Q.C. LAMAR
1883-93

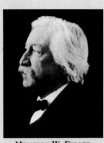

MELVILLE W. FULLER
1888-1910

Foreword

THIS FIFTH EDITION of *Equal Justice Under Law* is published by the Supreme Court Historical Society. Like the Society's other publications, this book is intended to broaden public awareness and understanding of the rich judicial heritage of the Supreme Court of the United States.

The Society publishes or sponsors a number of resources intended for researchers; *Equal Justice,* however, is aimed at a general audience. An interesting and informative overview of the history of the Supreme Court, it highlights the Justices and the major cases through which the Court has defined the Constitution over the past 200 years.

In many cases *Equal Justice* affords readers their first exposure to the Supreme Court's history and its integral role in our government's system of checks and balances. Since such information is critical to young Americans' understanding of our constitutional form of government, the Society vigorously promotes distribution of this book for use by high-school and college students. Thousands of copies have been placed in classrooms and libraries across the country through grants by foundations, state and local bar associations, and private donors. The American Bar Association's Public Education Division helped develop and publish a *Teacher's Guide* to *Equal Justice,* greatly enhancing the book's utility in secondary schools.

Equal Justice begins by comparing the Court's foundations with those of its European antecedents. Unlike the common-law courts of England and the civil-law courts on the Continent, which evolved over centuries, the Supreme Court of the United States was brought into being by Article III of the Constitution, just as Congress and the Presidency were created by Articles I and II, respectively. Under the powerful leadership of Chief Justice John Marshall, whose 34-year tenure began in 1801, the Court rapidly assumed its role as a coequal and independent branch of the federal government.

This book traces the Court chronologically from its beginnings in 1789, through landmark modern cases such as *Brown* v. *Board of Education* and *Roe* v. *Wade,* to important decisions of the 1987-88 term. It demonstrates the Court's influence in the evolution of the powers of the federal government and in social evolution affecting the day-to-day lives of every citizen.

Members of the Supreme Court staff, through the courtesy of Noel Augustyn, Administrative Assistant to the Chief Justice, were kind enough to review the new historical material. The Court's staff is not, however, responsible for the final text.

The need to understand the role of the Supreme Court has been present since the founding of the Republic. But not until 1965, under the sponsorship of the Foundation of the Federal Bar Association, was an authoritative presentation available to the public. The Foundation published three editions of this book; the Fourth Edition was published by the Supreme Court Historical Society with the Foundation's cooperation.

To make the first and subsequent editions possible, Dr. Melvin M. Payne, Chairman Emeritus, the late Chairman Dr. Melville Bell Grosvenor, and Gilbert Grosvenor, President and Chairman of the Board, have generously provided the resources of the National Geographic Society.

JUSTIN A. STANLEY, President
The Supreme Court Historical Society

The Supreme Court of the United States in Washington, D. C. —

A Heritage of Law

"WE ARE very quiet there, but it is the quiet of a storm centre. . . ." In these words Associate Justice Oliver Wendell Holmes—the Great Dissenter—described the Supreme Court of the United States in 1913. His words are just as true today. The winds of controversy have often swirled about the Court, its place in American government, and the 104 Justices who have made its decisions since the early days of the Republic.

"The Republic endures and this is the symbol of its faith."

Every system of justice has some kind of highest tribunal, some court of last resort, to give the final word on a case. But the Court gives the final word on a law, or on the powers of government under law, by the standards of the Constitution. Judicial review, scholars call it. Today some nations follow the American example, but when the Supreme Court developed this power it gave the world a new invention.

How the Court established this power in unlikely circumstances, how it has kept and used it, is the story of this book.

The men who gave us the Constitution and the Court began their work with a successful revolution. Captain Levi Preston fought at Lexington in 1775; he explained why 62 years later: "... what we meant in going for those red-coats was this: we always had governed ourselves, and we always meant to. They didn't mean we should."

In general, our legal tradition grows out

of the English tradition. But no English judge can say from the bench, as an American judge may say: "The law on the books says thus-and-so; but in spite of the fact that the legislature passed it in due form, this law is void—it is unconstitutional and therefore no law at all."

The English constitution has remained unwritten; it was, and still is, a mass of precedents, and of rules drawn from them. But in America the colonists got used to something else: the idea of one *written* agreement as the basis of government. In 1606 a charter from King James I outlined a plan of government for settlers in Virginia. Before the Pilgrims landed in 1620, they drew up the Mayflower Compact for themselves, with a solemn promise to make and obey "just and equal Laws" for the general good. Royal and proprietary colonies alike had their written charters.

THE COLONISTS came to think of these documents as sharing the sanctity of natural law, the supremacy of natural rights, the solidarity of human society. They were thinking of their charters as we think of our Constitution. Increasingly, many colonists came to regard Parliament's laws on colonial affairs as unjust, even tyrannical. They appealed to the principles of a higher law, which could nullify even Acts of Parliament. Finally, they appealed to arms—they fought the Revolution.

War brought victory; peace brought trouble. America's first constitution, the "Articles of Confederation and perpetual Union," set up a "firm league of friendship," a government so simple it didn't work. Each state kept its "sovereignty, freedom and independence," and every power not expressly given to Congress. That Congress, one house in which each state had one vote, had to rely on the states for soldiers or money or law enforcement. Often the states didn't cooperate.

Distressed, George Washington saw that the country had "thirteen heads, or one head without competent powers." John Jay warned in 1783 that Europe watched "with jealousy, and jealousy is seldom idle"—weakness at home might tempt assault from abroad. The states squabbled among themselves over trade; in 1786 James Madison wrote gloomily to Thomas Jefferson about the "present anarchy of our commerce." Protests grew sharper, until Congress reluctantly called for a convention to meet in Philadelphia in May, 1787, "for the sole and express purpose of revising the Articles of Confederation."

The delegates straggled in, elected Washington to preside, and with great courage and good sense disobeyed their instructions. They went to work to create a new government—"a *national* government . . . consisting of a *supreme* Legislative, Executive and Judiciary." Their splendid disobedience produced the Constitution of the United States. It was not the Articles they revised, it was the future.

They invented something new, a plan for power the world had never seen before, an intricate system with both the states and the central government dealing directly with the people.

After long angry debates they compromised on a new kind of Congress, with two houses. After more wrangles they accepted the idea of an executive, a President. Without any argument at all the delegates

"THE LAW, WHEREIN, AS IN A MAGIC MIRROR, *we see reflected not only our own lives,*" *noted Oliver Wendell Holmes, Jr.,* "*but the lives of all men that have been!*" *Visitors stand at the threshold of the Nation's citadel of law, the Supreme Court. The dome of the Capitol rises in the west.*

NATIONAL GEOGRAPHIC PHOTOGRAPHER JOSEPH J. SCHERSCHEL © N.G.S.

accepted the proposal for a Supreme Court. They agreed on the kinds of cases courts of the United States should try; when they disagreed over details for the lower courts, they left the matter up to the new Congress.

Soberly, for a long time, they thought about the most important problem of all. The country's simple government under the Articles had not worked well. Now the delegates were offering a complicated arrangement with many more points to quarrel about—who should make the final decision in disputes about the Constitution?

TO THIS QUESTION the delegates gave no final answer. But they adopted a sentence to make an answer possible: "This Constitution, and the Laws of the United States which shall be made in Pursuance thereof . . . shall be the Supreme Law of the Land. . . ."

Angry debates and even brawls accompanied the immediate question: Should the people accept this new system? Patrick Henry spoke the fears of many when he said, "it squints towards monarchy. Your President may easily become King."

And where was a bill of rights? Most of the states had one in their own constitutions, and saw dangers in a document that failed to provide a list of liberties. Pamphlets came thick and fast. Some cried:

> *That the convention in great fury*
> *Have taken away the trial by jury;*
> *That liberty of press is gone,*
> *We shall be hang'd, each mothers son. . . .*

For months the issue was uncertain, because nine of the original 13 states had to ratify the Constitution before it would become law. But by June 21, 1788, the ninth —New Hampshire—had acted.

In the First Congress, James Madison led in drafting amendments to protect the freedom and rights of the people; the states approved them promptly, and, by December 15, 1791, the Bill of Rights was in force.

Now a "more perfect Union" replaced the faltering "league of friendship," and the new nation began its great experiment of liberty under the law. The Supreme Court became the interpreter of the law—not because the delegates provided that it must, but because things worked out that way.

THE NINE MEMBERS *of the 1988 Supreme Court gather in the paneled and pilastered West Conference Room for an informal portrait. From left: Associate Justices John Paul*

Associate Justice William J. Brennan, Jr., says: ". . . the Founding Fathers knew better than to pin down their descendants too closely. Enduring principles rather than petty details were what they sought to write down. Thus it is that the Constitution does not take the form of a litany of specifics."

And so disputes over its meaning have continued. But Chief Justice John Marshall declared: "It is emphatically the province and duty of the judiciary department to say what the law is." He warned: "We must

Stevens, Sandra Day O'Connor, Harry A. Blackmun, Chief Justice William H. Rehnquist, Associate Justices William J. Brennan, Jr., Thurgood Marshall, Byron R. White, Anthony M. Kennedy, Antonin Scalia. The group meets for formal and informal portraits each time a new Justice joins the Court.

never forget that it is a *constitution* we are expounding . . . intended to endure for ages to come, and consequently, to be adapted to the various *crises* of human affairs."

Charles Evans Hughes, who would become Chief Justice himself, stated the Court's responsibility more bluntly in 1907: "We are under a Constitution, but the Constitution is what the judges say it is."

So the Judges find its words "loaded," as Associate Justice Byron R. White says today. For more than a century the Court has been deciding cases that twine about a single statement, Congress shall have the power to regulate commerce among the several states. On four simple words, "due process of law," the Court has written volumes.

Still, in dealing with constitutional problems, the Court is free to change its mind. Justices have overruled their predecessors and themselves, to correct a decision in the light of experience. They sit as "a kind of Constitutional Convention in continuous session," said Woodrow Wilson. Their

11

changing views have helped make the Constitution meet the needs of each successive generation. But again and again they have stirred up wrath and controversy.

Before he became Associate Justice, Robert H. Jackson pointed out that Supreme Court Justices derive their offices from the favor of Presidential appointment and Senate confirmation. And they are "subject to an undefined, unlimited, and unreviewable Congressional power of impeachment. . . . Certainly so dependent an institution would excite no fears. . . ."

And yet, he said, "this Court has repeatedly overruled and thwarted both the Congress and the Executive. It has been in angry collision with the most dynamic and popular Presidents in our history. Jefferson retaliated with impeachment; Jackson denied [the Court's] authority; Abraham Lincoln disobeyed a writ of the Chief Justice; . . .

Wilson tried to liberalize its membership; and Franklin D. Roosevelt proposed to 'reorganize' it."

You feel this timeless epic when you stand in the empty Courtroom today. Here the voices of famous lawyers seem to come out of the stillness—John Quincy Adams, formidable and old; Henry Clay, taking a pinch from the Judges' snuffbox; Daniel Webster, in his legendary tribute to his alma mater, Dartmouth—"a small college, and yet there are those who love it."

Here is great drama—a Dred Scott case inflaming the passions of a nation. And an attorney, mortally ill, who left a hospital bed to address the Court, then mustered strength to write thanking the Justices for their courtesy before he died the next day.

Here is intense emotion—Justice James M. Wayne during the Civil War years speaking for the Union when his state and his

12

THUNDEROUS ORATOR, *lawyer Daniel Webster argued the Dartmouth College case before the Supreme Court and won a landmark decision that protected private property rights and encouraged growth of business corporations in all branches of commerce and industry.*

When the Justices decided this case, they were performing the continuing function of the Court—to interpret the Constitution and to define the law of the land.

Every citizen has been affected by opinions of the Court since the early days of the Republic. "It passes on his property, his reputation, his life, his all," said Chief Justice John Marshall, who heard the Dartmouth College case.

Residents of Hanover, New Hampshire, stroll before Dartmouth Hall in this 1803 drawing (above left). When the state tried to turn Dartmouth from a privately owned college into a state university, the college filed suit and retained Webster, whose argument became legend. "The question is simply this," he contended: "Shall our state legislature be allowed to take that which is not their own . . . ?" No, said the Supreme Court, when it held for the first time that a charter of incorporation is a contract which no state has constitutional power to impair.

family disowned it. And a young lawyer standing wordless at three invitations to begin, finally managing to say, "Mr. Chief Justice, may I have a minute to compose myself? I'm scared to death."

Here are nine Judges whose Court is the arbiter of the American government—the umpire of the federal system. Their decisions represent a majority, if not all, of the members, but their awesome responsibility falls in the end on individual shoulders. As the late Associate Justice John Marshall Harlan explained: "Under his oath, each member of the Court must decide each case as if he were its only judge."

Here, in the richness of its past, the strong and clashing forces it must meet, the mystery it must foresee, is the most sedate and yet most dramatic of all the elements of government. Here, in short, is the Supreme Court of the United States.

At the Supreme Judicial Court of the
United States, begun and held at New York, (being
the Seat of the National Government) on the first Monday
of February, and on the first day of said month, Anno
Domini 1790. —————

Present.

The Honble. John Jay Esquire Chief Justice
The Honble. { William Cushing, and
{ James Wilson, Esqrs. } Associate Justices. —

This being the day assigned by Law, for commencing
the first Session of the Supreme Court of the United
States, and a sufficient Number of the Justices not
being convened, the Court is adjourned, by the Justices
now present, untill to morrow, at one of the clock in the af-
ternoon. —————

Tuesday, February 2nd. 1790. —————

Present.

The Honble. John Jay Esqr. Chief Justice.
The Honble. { William Cushing
{ James Wilson, and
{ John Blair, Esqrs. } Associate Justices

Proclamation

Decisions for Liberty

WHENEVER JUDGES, lawyers, and legal scholars gather and the talk turns to the Constitution and the men who made it the law we live by, one name inevitably enters the conversation: John Marshall of Virginia.

"My gift of John Marshall to the people of the United States was the proudest act of my life," said John Adams, the second President, years after he left office.

Adams not only chose Marshall for Chief Justice in 1801, he forced a reluctant Senate to confirm the appointment. He had every right to be proud.

Marshall asserted the Court's mightiest power and dignity in its first great crisis. His decisions set the course for a bold venture —a new republic's voyage to greatness among the nations of the world. At the Court today Justices and others still speak of Marshall as the "great Chief."

The Constitution called for a Supreme Court and a federal judiciary, but left it to Congress to spell out the details. Congress did so in the Judiciary Act of 1789. Connecticut's Oliver Ellsworth—later to serve four years as Chief Justice—led the drafting in committee. This law created 13 district courts in principal cities, with one judge apiece, and three circuit courts to cover the other areas of the eastern, middle, and southern United States. Above these it set the Supreme Court, with a Chief Justice and five Associates, as the only court of appeals.

For the first Chief Justice, President Washington picked John Jay, New York-born statesman and diplomat. The President weighed sectional jealousies and personal ability in selecting Associate Justices —John Blair of Virginia, William Cushing of Massachusetts, James Wilson of Pennsylvania, James Iredell of North Carolina, and John Rutledge of South Carolina. All had helped establish the Constitution.

But only three of the Judges had reached New York, a temporary capital city, in 1790, when the Court convened for the first time. Required by law to sit twice a year, it began its first term with a crowded courtroom and an empty docket. Appeals from lower tribunals came slowly; for its first three years the Court had almost no business at all.

Spectators at early sessions admired "the elegance, gravity and neatness" of Justices' robes. But when Cushing walked along New York streets in the full-bottom professional wig of an English judge, little boys trailed after him and a sailor called, "My eye! What a wig!" Cushing never wore it again.

In 1791, the Court joined Congress and the President at Philadelphia; it heard discussions of lawyers' qualifications, but little else. Still, other duties exhausted the Justices. The Judiciary Act of 1789 required them to journey twice a year to distant parts of the country and preside over circuit courts. For decades they would grumble, and hope Congress would change this system; but Congress meant to keep them aware of local opinion and state law.

Stagecoaches jolted the Justices from city to city. Sometimes they spent 19 hours a day on the road. North of Boston and in the South, roads turned into trails. Justice Iredell, struggling around the Carolinas and Georgia on circuit, and hurrying to Philadelphia twice a year as well, led the life of a traveling postboy. Finding his duties "in a degree intolerable," Jay almost resigned. Congress relented a little in 1793; one circuit trip a year would be enough.

Sensitive issues appeared in some of the Court's first cases. Its decision in *Chisholm*

FIRST OFFICIAL RECORD *of the Court contains an error in the first line—the word* "Judicial." *Authorities think the Clerk, a Massachusetts man, inserted it because the highest tribunal in his state was the "Supreme Judicial Court." The National Archives, custodian of such papers, has lent this document to the Court for public display.*

NATIONAL GEOGRAPHIC PHOTOGRAPHER JOSEPH J. SCHERSCHEL © N.G.S.

FIRST CHIEF JUSTICE, *John Jay opened the initial session of the Supreme Court on February 1, 1790. President George Washington had named the 43-year-old New York lawyer to head the highest tribunal in the land after Congress had set the number of Justices at six in 1789.*

"He was remarkable for strong reasoning powers, comprehensive views, indefatigable application, and uncommon firmness of mind," said one of Jay's friends. The Federalist statesman set lasting standards of judicial excellence during five years of service as Chief Justice. Jay's Court established an all-important precedent by refusing to advise the President on matters of law; to this day, the Court speaks only on specific cases that come before it for review.

At Washington's request, Jay, still Chief Justice, embarked upon a famous diplomatic mission to Great Britain in 1794 to settle quarrels over British troops in the Northwest and private debts to British creditors. The treaty that Jay negotiated preserved the peace when war might well have destroyed the new Nation.

Jay resigned as Chief Justice in 1795 and became Governor of New York, serving for two terms. His tenure on the bench launched a tradition of high-minded dignity that continues to distinguish the Supreme Court.

v. *Georgia* shocked the country. During the Revolution, Georgia had seized property from men loyal to the Crown. With a pre-Revolution claim on such an estate, two South Carolinians asked the Court to hear their suit against Georgia. It agreed, saying the Constitution gave it power to try such cases. But when the day for argument came in 1793, Georgia's lawyers did not appear. The Court gave its decision anyway, in favor of the South Carolinians.

Georgia raged; other states took alarm. They were trying to untangle finances still snarled from the war. If they had to pay old debts to "Tories" they might be ruined. They adopted the Eleventh Amendment, forbidding any federal court to try a lawsuit against a state by citizens of some other state. Thus the people overruled the Supreme Court for the first time, and established a far-reaching precedent of their own. They would give the ultimate decision on constitutional disputes.

War between Britain and France brought two more basic precedents. President Washington was working desperately to keep the United States neutral and safe; he sent the Court 29 questions on international law and treaties, and begged for advice. The Justices politely but flatly refused to help. Under the Constitution, they said, they could not share executive powers and duties, or issue advisory opinions.

To this day, the Supreme Court will not give advice; it speaks only on the specific cases that come before it.

But by its decision in *Glass* v. *Sloop Betsey,* in 1794, the Court did defend neutral rights and national dignity.

Defying the President's neutrality proclamation, French privateers were bringing captured ships into American ports. There French consuls decided if the ships were to be kept as lawful prize.

Betsey, Swedish-owned, had American cargo aboard when the French raider *Citizen Genet* caught her at sea and took her to Baltimore. Alexander S. Glass, owner of a share of the cargo, filed suit for his goods, but the district court in Maryland ruled that it could not even hear such cases.

With the prestige of the country at stake, the government quickly appealed to the

CUPOLA-CROWNED *Royal Exchange in New York City housed the first meeting of the Supreme Court. Justices deliberated on the second floor of the gambrel-roofed hall. A brick arcade shades the ground floor, an open-air market where Broad and Water Streets intersect. During the first term the Judges appointed a court crier and a clerk, and admitted lawyers to the bar, but heard no cases. After two sessions here, the Court reconvened in Philadelphia, the national capital until 1800.*

"UNCOMMONLY CROUDED," *reports the* New York Daily Advertiser *(right) of the scene at the Supreme Court's scheduled opening; curious spectators had to wait until the next day to see the Court formally convened. Widely reprinted, such accounts described the "novel experiment of a National Judiciary" for readers throughout the states. Last paragraph cites new location of the federal court that moved out of the Exchange to make room for the Justices.*

...and
...d reading.   Adjourned.

THE SUPREME COURT

Of the United States, convened yesterday in this city; but a sufficient number of the Judges not being present to form a quorum, the same was adjourned till this day one o'clock.

The Hon. John Jay, Chief Justice of the United States,

The Hon. William Cushing, and

The Hon. James Wilson, Assistant Justices, appeared on the bench.

John M'Kesson, Esq. acted as Clerk.

The Court Room at the Exchange was uncommonly crouded.—The Chief Justice and other Judges of the Supreme Court of this state; the Federal Judge for the District of New-York; the Mayor and Recorder of New-York; the Marshal of the district of New-York; the Sheriff, and many other officers, and a great number of the gentlemen of the bar attended on the occasion.

The Federal Court for the district of New-York will be opened this day, in the Consistory room opposite the Dutch Church in Garden-street.

B O

BOSTON,
Plymouth & Sandwich
MAIL STAGE,
CONTINUES TO RUN AS FOLLOWS:

LEAVES Boston every Tuesday, Thursday, and Saturday mornings at 5 o'clock, breakfast at Leonard's, Scituate; dine at Bradford's, Plymouth; and arrive in Sandwich the same evening. Leaves Sandwich every Monday, Wednesday and Friday mornings; breakfast at Bradford's, Plymouth; dine at Leonard's, Scituate, and arrive in Boston the same evening.

Passing through Dorchester, Quincy, Wyemouth, Hingham, Scituate, Hanover, Pembroke, Duxbury, Kingston, Plymouth to Sandwich. *Fare*, from Boston to Scituate, 1 doll. 25 cts. From Boston to Plymouth, 2 dolls. 50 cts. From Boston to Sandwich, 3 dolls. 63 cts.

.N. B. Extra Carriages can be obtained of the proprietor's, at Boston and Plymouth, at short notice.— ☞STAGE BOOKS kept at Boyden's Market-square, Boston, and at Fessendon's, Plymouth.

LEONARD & WOODWARD.

BOSTON, *November* 24, 1810.

"**CIRCUITS PRESS HARD** *on us all,*" *moaned Chief Justice John Jay. A 1789 Act of Congress, requiring Supreme Court jurists to preside twice a year over circuit courts scattered throughout the Union, meant months of rugged travel.*

Broadside (left) depicts one common mode of transportation. After jolting in a stagecoach many hours daily over savage roads of ruts and rocks or helping lift the stagecoach from quagmires of mud, the Justices passed restless nights in crowded way stations such as Fairview Inn on the Frederick road (above) near Baltimore, Maryland.

Battered and exhausted by the rigors of travel, Judges often arrived at the circuit courts too late or too sick to hold a session. Still, their visits served to acquaint the people with the new judiciary branch.

TATTERED *knee breeches of John Marshall, the Nation's fourth Chief Justice, reveal his lifelong habit of bedraggled dress. But his speech was always persuasive, his genial charm unfailing, in a courtroom or out of it. Here, at a Virginia tavern during his circuit-riding days, he holds dapper young lawyers spellbound for nearly an hour. One traveler said that to try to describe Marshall's eloquence "would be an attempt to paint the sunbeams." Injuries suffered in a stage-coach crash while on circuit hastened his death.*

19

Supreme Court. Try the case and give satisfaction, the Justices told the Maryland court; foreign consuls would not decide American claims. Europe heard this decision; and the United States became, as Washington hoped, "more respectable."

OLD DEBTS AND GRUDGES were troubling relations between the United States and Great Britain. President Washington sent Chief Justice Jay to London as a special minister to settle the quarrels, and Jay negotiated a treaty. When he returned, New York elected him Governor, and he resigned from the Court.

To succeed him Washington chose John Rutledge; the Senate rejected the nomination. Patrick Henry, now an old man, declined to serve, and Oliver Ellsworth of Connecticut then become Chief Justice.

The Jay Treaty infuriated Americans who thought it too favorable to Britain. Feeling still ran high in 1796 as the Court reviewed the case of *Ware* v. *Hylton*. Many British subjects had claims against Americans from contracts made before the Revolution, and treaty provisions required their payment.

In his only argument before the Supreme Court, John Marshall defended a Virginia law abolishing payments to British creditors; he lost. A treaty of the United States must override the law of any state, ruled the Justices. When the Nation pledges its word, it must keep faith—a landmark decision that has held for almost two centuries.

But two raucous choruses were shouting abuse at each other when the Court met at Philadelphia for the last time, in August,

1800. The government was moving to a new site by the Potomac, where no one had even planned a judiciary building. In 1801 Congress loaned the Court a little ground-floor room in the unfinished Capitol; it crowded the Justices for seven years.

Changing capitals was easier than changing the government. With vast excitement, the people were tussling with an issue the Constitution ignored; painfully, nervously, they were working out a two-party system.

Against the Federalists, "the good, the wise, and the rich," the party of Washington and Adams, stood the admirers of Vice President Thomas Jefferson—"the Man of the People." Calling themselves Republicans, the Jeffersonians wanted to give the people more of a voice in government; they praised the ideals of the French Revolution,

they had nothing but distrust for Britain.

During John Adams's term as President, the French insulted the administration from abroad and the Republicans criticized it at home. Federalists had run the new government from the first. They feared attacks on themselves as attacks on the new Constitution. Hearing French accents in every critical sentence, they passed the Sedition Act of 1798.

This law endangered anyone who spread "false, scandalous and malicious" words against the government or its officers, to "bring them...into contempt or disrepute." It would expire with Adams's term of office on March 3, 1801.

"Finding fault with men in office was already an old American custom," writes one historian; "indeed, it had become an

FRENCH FRIGATE L'Embuscade *sails past the Battery of New York City in this contemporary engraving. During President Washington's Administration, French raiders roamed off American coasts, seized merchant ships, and took them into port for French consuls to decide if they were lawful prize. This practice defied the authority of the United States and its right to maintain neutrality in the war between France and Britain. When the French privateer* Citizen Genet *(below left) captured a Swedish ship with American cargo, a federal district judge held that his court had no jurisdiction in the matter. By its 1794 decision in the case* **Glass v. Sloop Betsey,** *the Supreme Court declared that American courts would decide all cases within the American domain.*

essential part of the pursuit of happiness."

Supreme Court Justices presided at trials on circuit and sent Republican journalists to jail for sedition. But the Republicans kept on criticizing, and shouting "Tyranny!" The Federalists answered with furious cries of "Treason!"

In the 1800 elections the "Lock Jaw" Federalists were routed—"Mad Tom" Jefferson would be President, his followers would control Congress.

Gloomily, the Federalists hoped that judges could save the Constitution from these "radicals." Chief Justice Ellsworth was ailing; he resigned. Jay refused to serve again. So Adams gave his Secretary of State,

John Marshall, to the Supreme Court. In Congress, the lame-duck Federalists passed a law to reduce the Court's membership to five (one less Justice for a Republican President to name). Abolishing circuit duties for the Justices and providing other reforms, this law set up new circuit courts with 16 judges. Adams quickly made his appointments—the famous "midnight judges."

Enraged, one Republican from Kentucky called Adams's tactics "the last effort of the most wicked, insidious and turbulent faction that ever disgraced our political annals."

Jefferson took his oath of office on March 4, 1801. Without precedents and with passions running high, the Presidency and the

HOMES OF THE COURT: *Philadelphia's Independence Hall (left) sheltered the Judges for two days in 1791—all they needed for their February term. In August they met in Old City Hall (above, with cupola), which served them for a decade. Their first session in Washington, D.C., came in 1801.*

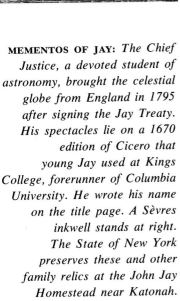

MEMENTOS OF JAY: *The Chief Justice, a devoted student of astronomy, brought the celestial globe from England in 1795 after signing the Jay Treaty. His spectacles lie on a 1670 edition of Cicero that young Jay used at Kings College, forerunner of Columbia University. He wrote his name on the title page. A Sèvres inkwell stands at right. The State of New York preserves these and other family relics at the John Jay Homestead near Katonah.*

JOE COVELLO, BLACK STAR

Congress passed for the first time from one party to another. And some citizens were afraid that the judiciary was in mortal danger.

Soon after his Inauguration, Jefferson wrote that the Federalists had "retreated into the judiciary as a stronghold, the tenure of which renders it difficult to dislodge them."

But the Republicans repealed the lame-duck Judiciary Act, while horrified Federalists lamented, "the Constitution has received a wound it cannot long survive," and "the angels of destruction . . . are making haste."

Meanwhile, William Marbury of Washington went straight to the Supreme Court, looking for a commission as justice of the peace for the District of Columbia. Adams had appointed 42 such officials, the Senate frantically confirmed them, and Adams sat at his desk until late on his last night in office to sign their commissions. Then a messenger rushed the papers to the State Depart-

"HILLS, VALLEYS, *morasses and waters," said Thomas Jefferson of the site chosen for Washington, here depicted in 1800. Stone bridge (center) spans Rock Creek near Georgetown (left). In background at right rises Jenkins Hill, where the Capitol stands today. The Senate and the House shared the old North Wing (below), first structure of the Capitol, with the Supreme Court. Here the Justices met in various rooms from 1801 until 1935. During the early years when construction displaced the Judges, they had to meet in nearby homes.*

ment for Marshall, still acting as Secretary, to affix the great seal of the United States. In the confusion some of the commissions went undelivered, Marbury's among them.

In December, 1801, Marbury applied to the Court for a writ of mandamus ordering James Madison, the new Secretary of State, to give him his commission. The Court agreed to hear the case—a bold action, for rumor was saying the Justices "must fall" by impeachment. Then the Republican Congress passed a law stopping the Court's sessions for 14 months: another threat. When the Justices finally sat again in 1803, they heard argument in Marbury's case.

If the Court ordered Madison to produce that commission, he could simply ignore the order; President Jefferson would defend him. If the Court denied Marbury's right to his commission, Jefferson could claim a party victory. Either way the Court's prestige—and perhaps its members—must fall.

Marshall found an escape from this dilemma. He announced the decision on February 24, and proclaimed the most distinctive power of the Supreme Court, the power to declare an Act of Congress unconstitutional. Point by point he analyzed the case. Did Marbury have a legal right to his commission? Yes. Would a writ of mandamus enforce his right? Yes. Could the Court issue the writ? *No.*

Congress had said it could, in the Judiciary Act of 1789. It had given the Court an original jurisdiction in such cases—power to try them for the first time. But, said Marshall triumphantly, the Constitution defined the Court's original jurisdiction and Congress could not change it by law. Therefore that section of the law was void.

The Court had issued such writs before, but Marshall ignored the fact. He declared for all time the supremacy of the Constitution over any conflicting law. Other judges had said as much, but Marshall added: "It is, emphatically, the province and duty of the judicial department, to say what the law is."

In renouncing a minor jurisdiction he asserted a great one, perhaps the greatest in the long annals of the law. The Supreme Court's power as interpreter of the Constitution rests on this precedent to this day.

A few days after the decision in *Marbury* v. *Madison,* the Court again amazed the Jeffersonians. They had passed a Judiciary Act in Congress, restoring the Court's old membership and circuit duties. The Justices ruled that it was constitutional, and for a while talk of impeachment died down.

"OYEZ! OYEZ! OYEZ!... the grand inquest of the nation is exhibiting to the Senate... articles of impeachment against Samuel Chase, Associate Justice...." The Supreme Court was on trial; if Chase fell, Marshall might be next.

Feared as a "ringleader of mobs, a foul mouthed and inflaming son of discord" when he led the Sons of Liberty in 1765, Chase "was forever getting into some... unnecessary squabble" as a Judge 40 years later. He campaigned openly for Adams. On circuit he tried Republicans without mercy. In 1803 he told a Baltimore grand jury that "modern doctrines" of "equal liberty and equal rights" were sinking the Constitution "into a mobocracy, the worst of all popular governments."

His enemies saw their chance. The House of Representatives voted to bring him before the Senate for trial, charging that his partisan behavior—in and out of court—amounted to "high Crimes and Misdemeanors" under the Constitution.

Vice President Aaron Burr had arranged a special gallery for ladies when the "grand inquest" opened on February 4, 1805. Burr had killed Alexander Hamilton in a duel and New Jersey wanted him for murder; but

he presided sternly, rebuking Senators who were eating cake and apples. "We are indeed fallen on evil times," said one. "The high office of President is filled by an *infidel;* that of Vice-President by a *murderer.*"

Representative John Randolph of Roanoke, the brilliant, erratic Virginian, fought to prove Chase unfit for the Court. Luther Martin of Maryland, who could hold more law and more brandy than any other attorney of his time, led Chase's defense. Marshall and 51 other witnesses testified.

Amid "a vast concourse of people... and great solemnity," the Senators acquitted

ON HIS LAST NIGHT *in the White House, President John Adams (right) sits up signing commissions for men of his party, the Federalists, defeated in the 1800 elections. But some of the papers went undelivered, including one to make William Marbury of Washington a justice of the peace. The victorious party of Thomas Jefferson, the Republicans, angrily called Adams's appointees "midnight judges"; political passion ran high when Marbury tried to claim his office by filing suit in the Supreme Court against James Madison, the new Secretary of State. Chief Justice Marshall avoided an open clash with Congress and the President. He found that the Court had no jurisdiction to order Marbury's commission delivered; although the Judiciary Act of 1789 said it did, the court held that provision of the law null and void. Thus for the first time, in* **Marbury v. Madison,** *the Supreme Court exercised its power to declare an Act of Congress unconstitutional. This was not the first example of judicial review—the Court had upheld a federal law as valid in 1796—but it remains the classic precedent for the Supreme Court's role as final interpreter of the Constitution.*

27

"**HIS BLACK EYES** . . . *possess an irradiating spirit, which proclaims the imperial powers of the mind that sits enthroned therein," a lawyer wrote of John Marshall, who posed for this portrait about a year before his death at 79. Still known as "the great Chief Justice," Marshall joined the Court in 1801 and presided for 34 years. The compelling force of his logic brought prestige to the judicial department. His far-sighted opinions, vitalizing the law to this day, helped mold the Nation by upholding the powers of the Union against claims for states' rights.*

Chase on March 1. Jefferson called impeachment of Justices "a farce which will not be tried again," and he was right.

For all his differences with the Republicans, John Marshall was no son of discord. Born in a log cabin near Germantown, Virginia, in 1755, he grew up near the frontier, with some tutoring for an education. He fought as an officer in the Revolution, almost freezing at Valley Forge.

After the war he practiced law, and became the leading Federalist of his state. As a young attorney and an aging Chief Justice, he was sloppily dressed and wonderfully informal out of court, fond of spending hours with friends in taverns, law offices, and drawing rooms. Even in his sixties, Marshall was still one of the best quoits players in Virginia.

When the Court met in Washington, the Justices stayed in a boardinghouse—the trip was too long, the session too short for their wives to accompany them—and Marshall's geniality brightened their off-duty hours.

Justice Joseph Story handed down a tale still told at the Court. On rainy days the Judges would enliven their conferences with wine; on other days Marshall might say, "Brother Story, step to the window and see if it doesn't look like rain." If the sun was shining, Marshall would order wine anyway, since "our jurisdiction is so vast that it must be raining somewhere."

Congress expanded that domain in 1807, creating a new circuit for Kentucky, Tennessee, and Ohio, and adding a seat to the Court. Jefferson appointed Thomas Todd, who had helped create the State of Kentucky out of his native Virginia.

LIFE IN WASHINGTON went on peacefully for months during the War of 1812. "Mrs. Madison and a train of ladies" visited the Supreme Court one day in early 1814, just as William Pinkney of Maryland, one of the country's most celebrated lawyers, was ending an argument; "he recommenced, went over the same ground, using fewer arguments, but scattering more flowers."

Rudely interrupting such diversions, the British arrived in August and burned the Capitol. Congress found shelter in the makeshift "Brick Capitol" where the Supreme Court Building stands today.

The Court, forced to shift for itself, met for a while in a house on Pennsylvania Avenue. Then it got temporary space in the Capitol. In 1819 it returned to its own semicircular room below the Senate Chamber.

"A stranger might traverse the dark avenues of the Capitol for a week," reported a visitor from New York, "without finding the

"I WAS . . . FLOORED," *says Marshall with dry humor as an attendant rushes to the sprawled Chief Justice, who fell from a stepladder in a law library. The mishap reveals Marshall's relish for a joke even at his own expense. He charmed even his critics with his "great good humour and hilarity." Marshall never allowed his mental powers to corrode. He had "one . . . almost supernatural faculty," wrote a lawyer, "that of developing a subject by a single glance of his mind. . . ."*

remote corner in which Justice is administered to the American Republic. . . ."

Strangers traversing the Republic had other troubles. "I passed away my 20-dollar note of the rotten bank of Harmony, Pennsylvania, for five dollars only," a disgusted traveler complained at Vincennes, Indiana. State-chartered banks, private banks, towns, sawmills, counterfeiters—all issued notes freely. "Engravings," a Scotsman called them; no law required anyone to accept them at face value as legal tender. Everyone suffered from this chaos.

Congress had chartered the second Bank of the United States in 1816 to establish a sound national currency, to issue notes it would redeem in gold or silver. By law, the government owned a fifth of the Bank's stock and named a fifth of its directors; private investors had the rest. Unscrupulous characters got control of the Bank and mismanaged its affairs.

In the South and West, where "engravings" flourished, the Bank's branches made bad loans until the home office at Philadelphia issued new orders in August, 1818: Call in those loans, don't accept any payments but gold and silver or our own notes. Panic spread. Local banks demanded payment on their own loans, and refused to extend credit; people scrambled for money they couldn't find; land went for a song at sheriffs' auctions; shops closed; men who lost their last five dollars said bitterly, "the Bank's saved and the people are ruined."

State legislators decided to drive the Bank's branches out of their domain. Maryland passed a tax law giving the Baltimore

JUDGE ON TRIAL: *White-haired Samuel Chase (seated in box at right) hears Representative John Randolph of Virginia accuse him of "high Crimes and Misdemeanors." The House impeached Chase, an outspoken Federalist, in 1805, after he used the bench of a circuit court to denounce Jeffersonian ideals of "equal rights."*

When the Senate acquitted Chase, Republicans gave up the idea of removing Federalist judges by such proceedings. Congress has never used its constitutional powers of impeachment against any other Justice of the Supreme Court.

31

branch its choice: pay up handsomely or give up and leave. The branch ignored it. Maryland sued the cashier, James McCulloch, and won in its own courts. McCulloch took his case—that is, the Bank's—to the Supreme Court, where argument began on February 22, 1819.

Splendid in his blue coat with big brass buttons, Daniel Webster spoke for the Bank —Congress has power to charter it; Maryland has no power to tax it, for the power to tax involves a power to destroy; and never, under the Constitution, may the states tax the Union into destruction.

Luther Martin, Maryland's Attorney General, argued for his state. Where does the Constitution say Congress has power to create a national bank? he asked. Nowhere! he thundered. It lists specific powers, and making banks is not one of them. Mr. Webster says it *implies* such a power. Nonsense!

For the Court, Marshall defined the controversy: "a sovereign state denies the obligation, of a law . . . of the Union." An "awful" question, but "it must be decided peacefully." Because the Union is "emphatically, and truly, a government of the people," it must prevail over the states. To specific powers of Congress, the Constitution adds power to make all laws "necessary and proper" for carrying them into effect.

Marshall invoked "letter and spirit" to give that clause its meaning: "Let the end be legitimate, let it be within the scope of the constitution," and Congress may use "all means which are appropriate . . . which are not prohibited." So the Bank was constitutional; no state might tax it. Maryland's law was "unconstitutional and void."

The Court's ruling settled the conflict of law but not the political fight over the Bank's power and states' rights. Virginia's legislature made a "most solemn protest" against the decision in *McCulloch* v. *Maryland;* Ohio officials took money by force from one Bank branch. Not until President Andrew Jackson vetoed the Bank's recharter did that controversy die down.

States' rights against the powers of the Union—the issue became more explosive

WILDCAT "ENGRAVINGS" *of dubious value issued by local banks underlie a five-dollar note from the second Bank of the United States, charted by Congress in 1816 to provide a sound currency. Caught without proper reserves during the financial panic of 1818, local banks had to foreclose on mortgages and auction land (left). People blamed banks in general, and the Bank in particular, for the severe depression that followed.*

Maryland and other states passed laws levying a heavy tax against the Bank's branches, hoping to close them. When cashier James McCulloch of the Baltimore branch ignored the law, Maryland sued him.

*The Constitution does not say Congress can charter a bank, argued the state (**McCulloch v. Maryland**). But the Supreme Court said the Bank was lawful, ruling for the first time that "implied powers" in the Constitution enable Congress to enact laws "on which the welfare of a nation essentially depends."*

than ever when the country faced its first great quarrel over slavery, in 1819. Southerners in Congress threatened secession and civil war; a Georgian foresaw "our houses wrapt in flames." When the House was discussing a bill to make Missouri Territory a state, a New York Representative had suggested that Congress forbid slavery there. Southerners warned, "the Union will be dissolved." The reply flashed, "let it be so!"

For months the furious debate went on. Then, in February, 1820, Senator Jesse B. Thomas of Illinois offered a compromise: Maine to be a free state; Missouri a slave state, and the rest of the Louisiana Purchase north of 36° 30′ free soil forever. Henry Clay supported the plan; early in March, President James Monroe signed the laws to carry it out. Apparently the crisis was over.

But trouble flared again as Congress debated Missouri's proposed constitution and states' rights in general, and what had been a trivial criminal case quickly became a rallying point for states' rights advocates and

proponents of secession. In Norfolk, Virginia, P. J. and M. J. Cohen were charged with violating a state law by selling six tickets in a lottery established by Congress to pay for improvements in the District of Columbia. The law forbade all lotteries except the state's own. A Norfolk court convicted the Cohens; they turned to the Supreme Court, pointing out that their lottery tickets were authorized by federal law.

Virginia rose in wrath. Her General Assembly declared that the Court had no

FRENZIED NORTHERNERS *carry the effigy of Pennsylvania Congressman David Fullerton toward a barrel of burning tar at the county courthouse in Carlisle. The angry crowd marched through the streets in protest of Fullerton's vote for the 1820 Missouri Compromise that enabled Missouri to join the Union as a slave state. Later Fullerton resigned as a result of the feeling. Such agitation over slavery in the territories made the Dred Scott case a national issue 37 years later.*

BITTER PARTNERS: *Aaron Ogden (left) sued Thomas Gibbons over steamboat shipping rights in New York's harbor (below), claiming exclusive rights under state law. But Gibbons insisted that an Act of Congress permitted his steamboats to enter; and the Supreme Court ruled in his favor. Former Justice Arthur Goldberg has said: "In* **Gibbons v. Ogden,** *Marshall gave the classic interpretation of the Constitution's commerce clause, which made the United States a common market."*

"DEVIL IN A SAWMILL!" *cried one startled rustic as Fulton's steamboat plied the Hudson River.*

jurisdiction. Her lawyers fought the Cohens' request for a hearing. They warned the Supreme Court against "exciting the hostility of the state governments," which would decide how long the Union should endure.

Then, in March, 1821, a second compromise was reached, bringing Missouri into the Union five months later as a slave state, but with guarantees designed to protect the rights of free Negroes and mulattoes. The issues of slavery and secession subsided, eventually to be resolved in blood.

Undeterred by the impassioned controversy, Marshall gave an uncompromising ruling on *Cohens* v. *Virginia.* The Court would hear the case; it existed to resolve such "clashings" of state and Union power, to keep the national government from becoming "a mere shadow." Insisting on the power of his Court, the Chief Justice boldly met the threat of secession and the claims of state sovereignty; he upheld the Union as the supreme government of the whole American people.

Then the Court heard argument on the merits of the case, and affirmed the sentence of the Norfolk court. The Cohens lost $100 — their fine — and costs.

SOUTHERNERS FUMED at Marshall's stand in the Cohens' case. But in 1824, for once, a Marshall ruling met popular acclaim. Huzzas from the wharves greeted the steamboat *United States* as she chuffed triumphantly into New York harbor, her crew firing a salute, her passengers "exulting in the decision of the United States Supreme Court." That case was *Gibbons* v. *Ogden.*

Robert Fulton successfully demonstrated a steampowered vessel on the Seine at Paris in 1803. With his

37

"INTEREST OF THE PUBLIC *must ...always be regarded as the main object" of charters, said Roger B. Taney. As Chief Justice he wrote this view into law in settling a controversy over two bridges at Boston. Proprietors of the Charles River toll bridge (right), under state charter, claimed Massachusetts could not let another company open a competing bridge nearby.*

In this clash of private rights and state powers, a new voice at the Supreme Court spoke for the community. In 1835, President Andrew Jackson had named Taney, his former Attorney General, to succeed Marshall as Chief Justice.

Taney lacked ornate eloquence, but his hollow, low voice and earnest delivery added clarity and persuasiveness to his statements. His defiant stand on citizens' rights during the Civil War brought him public scorn.

*In the bridge case, his first important opinion, Taney ruled that the state had power to approve construction of the much-needed Warren Bridge to serve the people. This decision (**Charles River Bridge v. Warren Bridge**) spanned a gap between established property rights and changing needs.*

CAUSEWAY OF CONTROVERSY: *Charles River Bridge in 1789 ran from the foot of Prince Street in Boston (foreground) to old*

partner, Robert R. Livingston, he held an exclusive right from New York's legislature to run steamboats on state waters, including New York harbor and the Hudson River. In 1807 their steamer splashed up the Hudson to Albany; soon money flowed into their pockets. Anyone else who wanted to run steamboats on those waters had to pay them for the privilege; some Albany men attacked the monopoly in state courts, and lost.

In 1811 the territorial legislature in New Orleans gave the partners a monopoly on the Mississippi. Now they controlled the two greatest ports in the country.

New Jersey passed a law allowing its citizens to seize steamboats owned by New Yorkers; other states enacted monopolies and countermeasures until the innocent

Charlestown, Massachusetts. The bridge, then considered a remarkable engineering feat, stretched 1,503 feet on 75 oak piers.

Despite predictions that strong tidal currents or floating ice would collapse the span, it stood more than a century.

side-wheeler was turning into a battleship.

Meanwhile three men of property went into business, then into rages, then into court. Robert Livingston's brother John bought rights in New York bay; then he sublet his waters to former Governor Aaron Ogden of New Jersey, a quarrelsome lawyer. Ogden took a partner, Thomas Gibbons, equally stubborn and hot tempered.

Under an old Act of Congress, Gibbons had licensed two steamboats for the national coasting trade, and now he invoked this federal law to get a suit against Ogden before the Supreme Court.

The once obscure Supreme Court was now a focus of public interest. Ladies crowded lawyers to hear the case. Daniel Webster spoke for Gibbons on February 4,

1824; Ogden's attorneys quoted established law and precedents for two days. But Marshall avoided shoals of precedents and veering winds of state laws to set his course by the Constitution—the clause giving Congress power to regulate commerce among the states. For the first time the Court defined these words; in them Marshall found vast new currents of national strength.

More than buying and selling, he proclaimed, commerce is intercourse among nations and states; it includes navigation. For all this rich activity Congress may make rules; if its rules collide with state restrictions the latter must sink. New York's law went down before an Act of Congress.

State monopolies could not scuttle ships "propelled by the agency of fire." Steam-

boats would be as free as vessels "wafted on their voyage by the winds."

With monopolies swept away, steamboat trade spread fast and freely. Soon, by that precedent, steam cars on rails spread across state lines, across the continent.

Marshall watched, as changes came and went. "We must never forget," he had said, "that it is a *constitution* we are expounding .... a constitution, intended to endure for ages to come, and consequently, to be adapted to the various *crises* of human affairs." His actions made his words unforgettable.

When Marshall gave the Presidential oath to his cousin Thomas Jefferson in 1801, the Supreme Court was a fortress under attack. It had become a shrine when he gave the oath to Andrew Jackson in 1829.

New crises arose during Jackson's Administration. Marshall carried on his work, concerned for the country's future but not for his failing health. Jay had resigned after five years, Ellsworth after four; Marshall served from 1801 until his death in 1835. When he took the judicial oath the public hardly noticed; when he died the Nation mourned him. "There was something irresistibly winning about him," said the *Richmond Enquirer.* And *Niles' Register,* which had long denounced his decisions, said, "Next to WASHINGTON, only, did he possess the reverence and homage of the heart of the American people."

BLOODSHED IN THE SENATE: *South Carolina Representative Preston Brooks flails Senator Charles Sumner of Massachusetts after Sumner has unleashed an antislavery speech insulting Brooks's cousin, Senator Andrew Pickens Butler of South Carolina. The attack occurred in 1856, during the crisis over expansion of slavery into Kansas. Although the Supreme Court tried to resolve the slavery issue, passions exploded into civil war.*

"WHIRLWIND OF MURDER," *wrote poet John Greenleaf Whittier of the Marais des Cygnes massacre. Near the Kansas border, proslavery riders shoot settlers who would vote for a free state in a fair election.*

About Marshall's successor, a New York journal sputtered: "The pure ermine of the Supreme Court is sullied by the appointment of that political hack, Roger B. Taney." Daniel Webster confided, "Judge Story. . . . thinks the Supreme Court is *gone*, and I think so too." The Senate debated the nomination for almost three months.

Born in Maryland in 1777, Taney attended Dickinson College, read law, and plunged into Federalist politics. While other lawyers took pride in oratory, he spoke simply in low tones that convinced juries.

Invoking freedom of speech, Taney won acquittal in 1819 for a Methodist preacher whose sermon on national sins provoked the charge of trying to stir up slave rebellion.

Suspicious of the Bank of the United

41

States, Taney campaigned for Andrew Jackson. In 1831 President Jackson wrote, "I have appointed mr Tauney atto. Genl." (His spelling gives the right pronunciation.) Taney supplied legal weapons in Jackson's war with the Bank, when passion ran so high that Vice President Martin Van Buren wore pistols to preside in the Senate.

Presiding over the Supreme Court for the first time, in January, 1837, Taney wore plain democratic trousers, not knee breeches, under his robe. The Court was entering a new era. A law passed in March added two new judicial circuits in the southwest and two Associate Justices. The Court be-

came unmistakably Jacksonian; conservatives dreaded what it might do to property.

But property survived. Its rights were "sacredly guarded," Taney wrote in the Charles River Bridge case, but "we must not forget that the community also have rights, and that the happiness and well being of every citizen depends on their faithful preservation." He interpreted corporation charters more strictly, state powers more generously, than Marshall had.

Meanwhile, a new agitation over human rights was growing. If it went on, wrote a Georgia planter, "we will be compelled to arm our Militia and shoot down our property

A PUBLIC MEETING

WILL BE HELD ON

THURSDAY EVENING, 2D INSTANT,

at 7½ o'clock, in ISRAEL CHURCH, to consider the atrocious decision of the Supreme Court in the

DRED SCOTT CASE,

and other outrages to which the colored people are subject under the Constitution of the United States.

C. L. REMOND,
ROBERT PURVIS,

and others will be speakers on the occasion. **Mrs. MOTT, Mr. M'KIM** and **B. S. JONES** of Ohio, have also accepted invitations to be present. All persons are invited to attend. Admittance free.

"ATROCIOUS DECISION," *cries a poster in Philadelphia, where abolitionists shouted their rage and disgust over the outcome of a famous Supreme Court case,* **Dred Scott v. Sandford.** *A slave in Missouri, Dred Scott sued for his liberty, insisting that a sojourn on free soil in Illinois and Wisconsin Territory entitled him to be free. In 1857, the Supreme Court rejected his claim. Chief Justice Taney said no Negro could be a citizen with constitutional rights to bring suit. His opinion wounded the Court's prestige in the North, for it insisted that Congress had no power to limit the expansion of slavery. Northern papers bristled with moral indignation; said one editorial, "If the people obey this decision, they disobey God."*

"**BID STRONG** *for this woman and child!*" *shouts a slave auctioneer on the steps of St. Louis's old courthouse. Here Dred Scott's case was first heard by state judges. It finally reached the Supreme Court. Federal marshals (right), acting under the 1850 Fugitive Slave Law, seize a Negro suspected of being a runaway slave.*

HOLCOMB

WISPY AND BENT, *Chief Justice Taney administers the Presidential oath of office to James Buchanan in 1857. In his Inaugural Address, Buchanan said the question of territorial slavery would "be speedily and finally settled" by the Supreme Court. Instead, Taney's ruling on Scott only sped the Civil War.*

"HEAP O'TROUBLE," *said Scott of his decade-long lawsuit. After the Supreme Court denied Scott freedom, his owner released him from bondage. Newspaper pictures him with wife and daughters.*

in the field. . . . tell the agitators we had rather fight them than our own negroes, and that we will do it too. . . ."

In 1846 the United States and Mexico went to war. A suit filed in a Missouri court by a Negro named Dred Scott went unnoticed. Twelve years earlier, John Emerson, an Army surgeon, had taken his slave Scott from Missouri to Illinois, where the Northwest Ordinance and state law forbade slavery. Then he had taken Scott to Fort Snelling, a frontier Army post in territory where the Missouri Compromise banned slavery forever. In 1838 he had taken Scott back to Missouri. Emerson died, and Scott sued the widow, claiming that this sojourn on free soil had made him a free man. In 1850 the Missouri court declared him free.

Mrs. Emerson appealed. The state's highest court ruled in 1852 that, free or not on free soil, Scott became a slave under state law when he went back to St. Louis.

Scott's was becoming a test case. To get it into a federal court—because federal courts have jurisdiction in suits between citizens of different states—title to Scott passed to Mrs. Emerson's brother, John F. A. Sanford of New York (misspelled "Sandford" in the records).

Claiming Missouri citizenship, Scott sued Sanford for his freedom in the federal court in St. Louis. Sanford's lawyers argued that Scott could not be a citizen because he was a slave and a Negro. The court ruled against Scott on May 15, 1854.

Congress passed the Kansas-Nebraska Act two weeks later, opening areas of the West to slavery where it had been banned by the Missouri Compromise. Furious northerners burned its author, Stephen A. Douglas, in effigy. On July 4, abolitionist William Lloyd Garrison publicly burned a copy of the Constitution, crying, "So perish all compromises with tyranny."

Fighting broke out in Kansas and made the expansion of slavery the issue in the 1856 Presidential campaign, won by James Buchanan. The Supreme Court heard argument in *Dred Scott* v. *Sandford* in February, 1856, reached the end of its term, then heard argument again in December.

By then the whole country had heard of Dred Scott. "The Court, in trying this case, is itself on trial," said the *New York Courier.*

In February, 1857, a majority of the Justices agreed to follow precedent and say that the ruling of the highest state court was final—that Scott was a slave under state

FRANK LESLIE'S ILLUSTRATED NEWSPAPER

Entered according to Act of Congress, in the year 1857, by FRANK LESLIE, in the Clerk's Office of the District Court for the Southern District of New York. (Copyrighted June 22, 1857.)

No. 82.—VOL. IV.]　　　　NEW YORK, SATURDAY, JUNE 27, 1857.　　　　[PRICE 6 CENTS.

TO TOURISTS AND TRAVELLERS.

We shall be happy to receive personal narratives, of land or sea, including adventures and incidents, from every person who pleases to correspond with our paper.

We take this opportunity of returning our thanks to our numerous artistic correspondents throughout the country, for the many sketches we are constantly receiving from them of the news of the day. We trust they will spare no pains to furnish us with drawings of events as they may occur. We would also remind them that it is necessary to send all sketches, if possible, by the earliest conveyance.

VISIT TO DRED SCOTT—HIS FAMILY—INCIDENTS OF HIS LIFE—DECISION OF THE SUPREME COURT.

WHILE standing in the Fair grounds at St. Louis, and engaged in conversation with a prominent citizen of that enterprising city, he suddenly asked us if we would not like to be introduced to Dred Scott. Upon expressing a desire to be thus honored, the gentleman called to an old negro who was standing near by, and our wish was gratified. Dred made a rude obeisance to our recognition, and seemed to enjoy the notice we expended upon him. We found him on examination to be a pure-blooded African, perhaps fifty years of age, with a shrewd, intelligent, good-natured face, of rather light frame, being not more than five feet six inches high. After some general remarks we expressed a wish to get his portrait (we had made efforts before, through correspondents, and failed), and asked him if he would not go to Fitzgibbon's gallery and

have it taken. The gentleman present explained to Dred that it was proper he should have his likeness in the "great illustrated paper of the country," overruled his many objections, which seemed to grow out of a superstitious feeling, and he promised to be at the gallery the next day. This appointment Dred did not keep. Determined not to be foiled, we sought an interview with Mr. Crane, Dred's lawyer, who promptly gave us a letter of introduction, explaining to Dred that it was to his advantage to have his picture taken to be engraved for our paper, and also directions where we could find his domicile. We found the place with difficulty, the streets in Dred's neighborhood being more clearly defined in the plan of the city than on the mother earth; we finally reached a wooden house, however, protected by a balcony that answered the description. Approaching the door, we saw a smart, tidy-looking negress, perhaps thirty years of age, who, with two female assistants, was busy ironing. To our question, "Is this where Dred Scott lives?" we received, rather hesitatingly, the answer, "Yes." Upon our asking if he was home, she said,

"What white man arter dad nigger for?—why don't white man 'tend to his own business, and let dat nigger 'lone? Some of dese days dey'll steal dat nigger—dat are a fact."

ELIZA AND LIZZIE, CHILDREN OF DRED SCOTT.

DRED SCOTT. PHOTOGRAPHED BY FITZGIBBON, OF ST. LOUIS.　　　HIS WIFE, HARRIET. PHOTOGRAPHED BY FITZGIBBON, OF ST. LOUIS.

FRANK LESLIE'S ILLUSTRATED NEWSPAPER (BELOW) AND LIBRARY OF CONGRESS

AMID FLYING STONES *and bullets the first Civil War victims fall during a riot in Baltimore in 1861. Southern sympathizers attacked the 6th Massachusetts Regiment, killing four soldiers. Loyal Unionists (left) guarded the office of the city's provost marshal against the mob. The military arrested citizens suspected of disloyalty, rebellion, or treason— including John Merryman, a prominent figure in Baltimore. In Merryman's behalf, Chief Justice Taney sent Lincoln a sharp official protest denying that the President had constitutional power to suspend the protection of law, especially the writ of habeas corpus, in any emergency whatsoever.*

REGIMENTAL COLOR *of the 6th Massachusetts heralded the unit on its way to Washington. The Baltimore rioters struck the militia April 19, 86 years to the day after Massachusetts Minutemen became the first Revolutionary War victims.*

law. Such a narrow finding would leave unresolved two dangerously controversial issues: Whether or not a free Negro might be a citizen of the United States; and whether or not the 1820 Missouri Compromise was constitutional.

When it was learned that two dissenting Justices planned to argue that Congress in fact had the power to regulate slavery in the territories, that under the Missouri Compromise Scott was a free man and a citizen, the majority decided to enlarge the scope of the decision and deny the power to Congress. Some members hoped the Court's opinion would resolve the question, win acceptance, and possibly save the Union.

Newly elected President James Buchanan may have shared that hope; in his Inaugural Address on March 4, he promised that "in common with all good citizens" he would "cheerfully submit" to the Court's decision.

Two days later the Justices began to deliver eight separate opinions. The majority ruled that Scott was still a slave. Three, including Taney, said no Negro, even if free, could hold citizenship in the United States.

And for the first time since 1803, the Court held an Act of Congress null and void. Under the Constitution, it announced, Congress had no power to limit the expansion of slavery by law, as the Missouri Compromise of 1820 had done.

Hopes that the decision would temper the confrontation were shattered by attacks on the Court from the abolitionist press and antislavery leaders—attacks that have never been surpassed in bitterness. Almost unnoticed, Scott's owner set him free. Before

47

the case was decided, Sanford had gone insane; before the slavery question was settled, more than 600,000 Americans would lose their lives in civil war.

"HAVE WE EVER had any peace on this slavery question?" asked Abraham Lincoln. The Illinois crowd yelled "No!" It was 1858; Lincoln was challenging Stephen A. Douglas for a Senate seat—and challenging the Supreme Court's ruling on slavery.

Douglas defended the decision in Dred Scott's case as the pronouncement of "the highest tribunal on earth," in spite of his own objections to it. "From that decision there is no appeal this side of Heaven," he cried.

One decision settles one case, retorted Lincoln; it does not even settle the law, still less the future of the country.

Douglas won the Senate seat; in 1860 he lost the race for the Presidency, and the Republicans came to power with Lincoln.

Chief Justice Taney administered the oath of office to Lincoln on March 4, 1861, and heard him disclaim "any assault upon the Court." But Lincoln warned solemnly: "if the policy of the Government, upon vital questions affecting the whole people, is to be irrevocably fixed by decisions of the

Supreme Court, the instant they are made, in ordinary litigation...the people will have ceased to be their own rulers. . . ."

That day the first banner of the Confederate States of America flew over the statehouse at Montgomery, Alabama.

Secession divided the Supreme Court. Justice John A. Campbell, who thought disunion wrong, resigned and went sadly home to Alabama. Justice James Moore Wayne of Georgia, last survivor of Marshall's Court, remained; until his death in 1867, he voted to sustain all the war measures the Court passed judgment on.

In Maryland, part of Taney's circuit, many favored the Union, some the South. Washington's only railroad to the north ran through Baltimore, where an angry crowd mobbed troops hurrying to defend the capital. Lincoln told the Army to suspend the writ of habeas corpus and establish martial rule, if necessary, to keep Maryland safe.

The military jailed citizens on mere suspicion; troops arrested John Merryman for taking part in the Baltimore riot and blowing up railroad bridges. Locked up in Fort McHenry, he applied for a writ of habeas corpus—a court order for proof that a prisoner is lawfully confined.

FAMOUS AUTHOR, *lawyer Richard Henry Dana, Jr., who wrote* Two Years Before the Mast, *defended Lincoln's blockade of southern coasts in the 1863 Prize Cases.*

GUNS BLAZING, *Union ships (above) chase a southern side-wheel steamer. A gun crew (below) prepares to fire a warning shot across the bow of another blockade runner. In 1861 Lincoln had blockaded southern ports. Owners of captured merchant ships and cargo, protesting that the Union sea barrier was unlawful, brought suit to recover their property. They argued that until Congress voted a declaration of war, Lincoln had no constitutional power to order a blockade. But in the Prize Cases, the Supreme Court upheld the President's bold acts. He had to fight the war, it said, "without waiting for Congress to baptize it with a name."*

49

Only in "Rebellion or Invasion" when "the public safety may require it" may the privilege of habeas corpus be suspended, says the Constitution.

Hurrying to Baltimore, Chief Justice Taney issued a writ to Gen. George Cadwalader: Bring Merryman to court and explain his arrest. The general sent a letter—he had to consult the President. Taney ordered a marshal to seize the general; but a sentry barred the marshal from Fort McHenry. The Chief Justice challenged the President's right to take legislative and judicial power, calling on him to uphold the law and the courts.

Lincoln did not reply; Congress upheld him. But when the emergency had passed, the government quietly brought Merryman's case to a federal court; later still, it quietly let him go free.

Resignation and death left three seats vacant at the Supreme Court. Lincoln appointed Noah H. Swayne of Ohio, Samuel F. Miller of Iowa, and his old friend from Illinois, David Davis. But no one knew what the Court would do when it heard the Prize Cases in 1863.

Before calling Congress into special session, Lincoln had authorized martial rule in Maryland, called for volunteers, pledged government credit for huge sums, and proclaimed a blockade of southern ports. To meet the crisis of war, the President swept into the realm of legislative power like an invading general. A legal battle over four merchant ships seized under Lincoln's blockade orders tested his actions before the Supreme Court.

The owners brought suit for the vessels and cargo, arguing that war alone warrants

"GUILTY!" *ruled this Civil War military commission that tried Lambdin P. Milligan, an Indiana lawyer, for conspiring to overthrow the government of the Union. A civilian, he demanded jury trial in a federal court.*

MILITARY COMMISSION THAT TRIED INDIANA CONSPIRATORS IN 1864.

GEN. S. COLGROVE. COL. T. LUCAS. COL. T. BENNETT   COL. B. SPOONER COL. D. DEHART MAJOR H. BURNETT

COL. STEVENS COL. WM. McLANE   COL. MURRAY   COL. R. WILLIAMS   COL. WM.   LIEUT. COL. HEATH

a blockade and only Congress may declare war; they denied that Lincoln's emergency powers had any reality in constitutional law.

If the Court upheld the blockade as a legal war measure, England and France might recognize the Confederacy; if it did not, the government would have to pay huge damages for captured ships, and other war measures would be in question. Either decision would endanger the Union.

Justice Robert C. Grier spoke for himself, Wayne, and Lincoln's three appointees: The President had to meet the war as "it presented itself, without waiting for Congress to baptize it with a name"; and rebellion did not make the South a sovereign nation. Four dissenters said the conflict was the President's "personal war" until Congress recognized the insurrection on July 13, 1861. But the prairie lawyer had won his case.

Chief Justice Taney died, aged 87, in October, 1864. Lincoln's Attorney General Edward Bates wrote that his "great error" in the Dred Scott case should not forever "tarnish his otherwise well earned fame." And not long after Taney's death, victory for the Union brought vindication of his defiant stand for the rule of law.

Army authorities had arrested Lambdin P. Milligan of Indiana, a civilian, tried him before a military commission, convicted him of conspiring to overthrow the government, and sentenced him to hang. With Milligan's petition for a writ of habeas corpus, the Supreme Court considered the problem of military power over civilians.

During "the late wicked Rebellion," Lincoln had authorized such military tribunals. But, said the Justices, the federal courts in Indiana were always open to try

*In 1866, the Supreme Court (**Ex parte Milligan**) held that no military tribunal could try civilians where federal courts were "open and ready to try them" because the Constitution protects "all classes of men, at all times, and under all circumstances."*

LAMBDIN P. MILLIGAN

THE COPPERHEAD PARTY.—IN FAVOR OF A VIGOROUS PROSECUTION OF PEACE!

TREACHEROUS COPPERHEADS, *members of a northern political faction that sought Civil War peace at any price, threaten the Union in this 1863 cartoon from* Harper's Weekly. *A southern sympathizer, Milligan plotted with other Copperheads to raid state and U. S. arsenals for a supply of weapons, free captured Confederate soldiers from northern prison camps, arm them, and send them back to fight for the South again.*

LAST SUPREME COURT CHAMBER *in the Capitol receives a famous advocate, retired Justice Stanley Reed, who in 1965 shows his grandchildren, Walter and Harriet Reed, where the Court met from 1860 to 1935. "I was admitted to practice before the Supreme Court on April 4, 1924," he recalls. "The first important case I argued for the government as Solicitor General was here in this room."*

As do all Solicitors General, he performed the duty of deciding which lower court decisions the government would appeal to the Court, what legal stand the government would adopt, and who would argue for the U.S. Reed joined the Court as an Associate Justice in 1938, and served until 1957. Below, in 1888, Chief Justice Morrison R. Waite presides over a Court session in this same room, the old Senate Chamber, sketched for Harper's Weekly.

cases like Milligan's. Therefore, under the Constitution, no military courts could try them; and, however shocking the charges, the defendants kept their rights under law.

At liberty again, Milligan sued the military for false imprisonment, and a jury awarded him damages—five dollars.

"WHAT a potato hole of a place, this!" A western lawyer, seeing the Court's first-floor room in the Capitol in 1859, thought the Justices should be "got up above ground" for some fresh air and daylight. In December, 1860, they finally moved to their new courtroom, the old Senate Chamber. With 12 rooms for their officials and records, they had more space than ever before.

Congress added a tenth seat to the Court

in 1863, and Lincoln appointed Stephen J. Field of California. To succeed Taney in 1864, he chose Salmon P. Chase of Ohio.

Ambitious and able, Chase had won fame for defending runaway slaves, served one term in the Senate and two as Governor of Ohio when Lincoln named him Secretary of the Treasury in 1861. Inexperienced in finance, Chase grappled with war costs— more than $1,000,000 a day. He planned a radical new tax on income, a new system of national banks. But plans for legal tender notes, the famous "greenbacks," upset him. War or no war, he thought, the Constitution forbade such paper money.

Lincoln sent Chase a message "not to bother himself about the Constitution. . . . I have that sacred instrument here at the

White House, and I am guarding it with great care." Reluctantly, Chase agreed.

Gossip described him addressing a mirror: "President Chase." His own hopeful publicity described his qualifications for Lincoln's place in 1864; the people declined his offer, and in June Lincoln accepted his resignation from the Treasury. Then Chase found himself named Chief Justice by the Chief Executive he had tried to supplant.

Under Radical Republican leaders, the postwar Congress seemed determined to reconstruct the whole American government. One Representative talked of an amendment to abolish the Supreme Court; another warned President Andrew Johnson "that as Congress shall order he must obey."

Striking at Johnson, Congress lowered the number of Justices from ten to eight; and to protect the Reconstruction laws, it limited the Court's jurisdiction on appeals.

It was the Senate, not the Court, that tried the most dangerous case of those bitter years, the impeachment of the President.

Johnson's political enemies wanted a quick conviction. The Constitution, however, required the Chief Justice to preside; and Chase insisted on presiding as a judge, while the Senate tried legal issues as a court should. The Radicals had to let him rule on points of law; Chase gave the President's lawyers a chance to be heard. Johnson escaped conviction by one vote.

Those same bitter years saw amendments altering the Constitution. In 1865 the Thirteenth abolished slavery; in 1868 the

IMPEACHED PRESIDENT *Andrew Johnson faced Radical Republicans' charges of "high Crimes and Misdemeanors" for ordering Edwin M. Stanton dismissed as Secretary of War. Chief Justice Chase (below) swears in Senator Ben Wade as impeachment court member. If Johnson had been convicted, Wade, as President pro tem of the Senate, would have succeeded him as Chief Executive.*

"FEAR NOT ... to acquit him," urged lawyer Henry Stanbery (standing at left, above) for President Johnson at his impeachment trial in 1868. Here Stanbery addresses Chief Justice Chase (on dais). As prosecutors, Managers for the House of Representatives sit at right. Former Associate Justice Benjamin R. Curtis (seated, center of table at left) argued that Johnson had not violated the Tenure of Office Act, which restricted removal of cabinet officers, and that the Act itself was invalid. Johnson escaped conviction by one vote. In 1926 the Supreme Court said the Act had been unconstitutional.

Fourteenth defined United States citizenship and defended it against infringements; in 1870 the Fifteenth barred racial limits on the right to vote.

Gen. Ulysses S. Grant became President in 1869. Congress raised the number of Justices back to nine, and at long last revised the circuit court system.

WHILE the South struggled with carpetbaggers and Ku Klux Klansmen, the rest of the country rushed into the splendors and scandals of the Gilded Age. Wartime greenbacks went cheap and debtors liked them; creditors wanted gold, and Chase and his Associates had to bother themselves about currency and the Constitution.

Hepburn v. *Griswold,* a private lawsuit, came before them in 1867, challenging the Legal Tender Act of 1862 and the Nation's money. Justice Wayne had died; when the remaining Judges discussed the case they divided four to four, as sharply as the rest of the country. Chase was one of those who opposed the law. If you had promised in 1861 to pay a debt in gold, he said, you could not force greenbacks on your creditor; Congress could not impair such contracts.

Then Grier, aged and sadly feeble, changed his vote so that Chase spoke for a majority. Somewhat awkwardly, the Chief Justice struck down in 1870 the law he had reluctantly defended at the Treasury.

Dissenting, Justice Miller insisted: Congress had all the powers it needed to fight a war, including power to change the currency.

Although the Court's decision applied to contracts made before February 25, 1862,

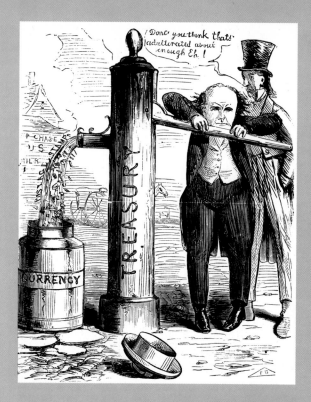

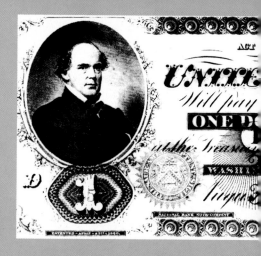

it implied that greenbacks might not be valid for later contracts. It called in question more than $350,000,000 in greenbacks. The government fretted. A Boston newspaper protested bitterly against "the country's being mangled and slaughtered, while the Supreme Court is making experiment upon the laws of currency."

Grier had resigned; Grant named William Strong and Joseph P. Bradley to the Court. They wanted to hear argument in other legal tender cases; astonished lawyers heard the Justices argue furiously on the bench about reopening the money question. After hearing the new cases in 1871, the two new Justices joined the three dissenters of *Hepburn* to overrule that decision.

Strong announced that the Legal Tender Act was constitutional; it helped pay for the war, it saved the Nation. Bradley, concurring, went further: Under the monetary power, Congress could provide for paper money even in peacetime emergencies—a view the Court accepted 13 years later.

Angry editors charged that Grant had packed the Court; and even people who liked greenbacks disliked the Court's reversing itself so thoroughly and so fast.

After the spring term of 1873, Chase died. A Negro guard of honor brought his casket to the Supreme Court Chamber for a state funeral. As it rested on Lincoln's catafalque, a moment of Presidential honor came to the Chief Justice at last.

FOR CHASE'S SUCCESSOR, the Senate confirmed Grant's nomination of Morrison R. Waite in 1874. Thoroughly respectable, this 57-year-old attorney from Ohio lacked the nationwide fame of Jay or Marshall or Taney or Chase.

"I am getting the hang of the barn a little," Waite wrote modestly after a week in Washington. By 1877, when he gave the Court's decision in the Granger cases, he had gotten it thoroughly.

Corn in the woodbox fed the political prairie fire of the Granger movement. Railroads were charging so much to ship grain that farmers burned it for fuel instead of

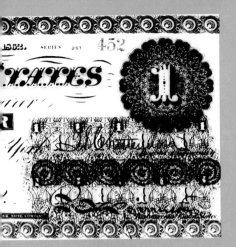

THE ONLY CHANGE *he could get, man at right laments during the 1863 money crisis. Meanwhile, the "greenback" (above) helped pay for Union war costs; the Court eventually held such legal tender notes valid in war or peace.*

sending it for sale. Joining the Grange, or Patrons of Husbandry, farmers took their wrongs to their legislatures; four states limited freight rates by law.

Illinois farmers had unexpected allies, merchants from the Chicago Board of Trade, so disgusted at sharp practices in the grain storage business that they were willing to fight for state regulation. When Illinois law set standards for warehousing, the firm of Munn & Scott was in trouble.

With huge grain elevators in Chicago, Ira Y. Munn and George L. Scott had piled up a fortune, a name for crooked dealings, a lot of enemies, and bankruptcy.

Used to charging what the traffic would bear, the railroads found state regulation unbearable; they took their wrongs to court.

When state and federal judges upheld the "Granger laws," railroad attorneys steamed hopefully to the Supreme Court, quoting the Fourteenth Amendment on due process of law, the contract clause, and the interstate commerce clause of the Constitution. With them went lawyers for the ruined Ira Munn,

still fighting a $100 fine for illegal storage rates. If these laws stood, they argued, private property would be wrecked.

Seven Justices found all these laws valid. Like Taney, they thought community rights as sacred as corporation rights. "For us the question is one of power," said Waite; when private property affects the community, the public has constitutional power to protect its interest by law, for the common good. Firms like Munn & Scott had virtual monopolies on grain—so Illinois could exercise its power to regulate them.

Waite assigned a modest role to the courts; they must assume that a legislature knows the facts, they must accept the legislature as "the exclusive judge" of when to pass regulatory laws and what to say in them.

The railroads contended that only Congress could regulate their trade; Waite ruled that until Congress did, the states were free to act within their own borders.

The *New York Herald* said: "either the people would govern the railroads, or the railroads would govern the people. The Su-

57

preme Court has come to the rescue. . . ."

But Justice Field, dissenting, called the decisions "subversive of the rights of private property." And his dissent would become the majority opinion in later decisions.

The railroads had rushed beyond state borders and laws, and Congress took action. It passed the Interstate Commerce Act in 1887, the Sherman Anti-Trust Act in 1890. Other laws—national and state—to regulate business and working conditions followed as time went by. But time proved that the legislatures were not to be the "exclusive judge." The Supreme Court began to set new limits on state power, although it did not flatly overrule the Granger decisions.

The Court also checked Congressional power. In 1895, a depression year, critics charged that the Court let property rights govern law. Waite had died, Melville W. Fuller had succeeded him as Chief Justice;

of the Court that decided *Munn* v. *Illinois* in 1877, only Field survived.

When the Court decided its first antitrust case, the government lost its suit against a company controlling some 98 percent of all sugar refined in the United States. The Court conceded that the trust had a monopoly on making "a necessary of life" but denied that it had a direct effect on interstate commerce. This ruling left the Sherman Act weak, the trusts as strong as ever.

In another case, the Court incurred the wrath of unionized labor. Federal judges, under the Sherman Act, had issued a sweeping injunction against union leaders of the Pullman strike in 1894. Jailed for contempt of court, Eugene V. Debs applied to the Supreme Court for a writ of habeas corpus; the Justices denied it unanimously.

In a third case, the Court heard argument on a new federal income tax law, which took two percent of all incomes over $4,000. Famous lawyers prophesied communism, anarchy, and despotism if the law survived. With one Justice ill, the rest divided four to four on most of the law's provisions. After reargument a five-to-four vote made the entire law unconstitutional.

Bluntly, the dissenters called this decision "the most disastrous blow ever struck at the constitutional power of Congress," "a surrender of the taxing power to the moneyed class." John Marshall Harlan (whose grandson of the same name was to serve on the Court in the 20th century) spoke out so sharply that the *New York Sun* called his "tone and language more appropriate to a stump address."

On the stump, William Jennings Bryan said the Court stood with the rich against the poor; other political figures took up the charge. And in 1913 the Sixteenth Amendment made the income tax constitutional after all.

U NDER THE CIVIL RIGHTS ACT of 1875, designed to prevent discrimination in public places, Negro citizens brought cases before the Court, protesting their exclusion from a hotel dining room in Topeka, an opera house in New York, the dress circle of a San Francisco theater, the ladies' car on a train. In 1883, eight Justices held the act unconstitutional. The Fourteenth Amendment, they said, only gave Congress power over state action; if private citizens discriminated among one another, Congress could do nothing about it. Harlan of Kentucky, the Court's only southerner, wrote a fighting 36-page dissent.

WAREHOUSES OF GRAFT: *Chicago grain elevators of Ira Munn and George Scott loom above the Chicago River. When Munn ignored an 1871 Illinois law that curbed high storage and railway shipping rates, the state sued. The Supreme Court ruling (***Munn v. Illinois***) upheld state power to regulate businesses "affected with a public interest."*

CHAMPION OF FARMERS, *the Grange wakes the public to corrupt railroad practices. Hard-hit by low grain prices, oppressed by high railroad and warehouse rates, farmers joined the Grange to protest their wrongs and fight for laws in their interest.*

To enforce segregation by color, southern states began passing Jim Crow laws, to require equal but separate passenger cars on trains. Homer Adolph Plessy challenged the Louisiana law in 1892, and took his case to the Supreme Court. Its opinion cited many state precedents to show the "reasonableness" of such laws, and found nothing to stamp "the colored race with a badge of inferiority." Harlan dissented again.

"Our Constitution is color-blind," he wrote. "In respect of civil rights, all citizens are equal before the law." Still, the separate-but-equal doctrine of *Plessy* v. *Ferguson* controlled the law for years.

THE SPANISH-AMERICAN WAR gave the United States several heroes, including Col. Theodore Roosevelt; many islands, including Puerto Rico and the Philippines; and one baffling question: Does the Constitution follow the flag? Across the American West, it always had; pioneers took their citizenship with them, and new states joined the Union as equals.

These new islands—separate by ocean, alien by culture—seemed unfit for self-government or statehood. But the Constitution said nothing about colonies of subject peoples, unequal before the law.

In the famous "Insular Cases" the Supreme Court worked out a constitutional status for the new possessions; in effect and by necessity, the Court made law as it went along. Spectacular as the subject was, the Justices were doing the duty of every judge, applying the generalities of law to the demands of the specific case.

In 1898, a case involving cast-iron pipe ushered in a decade of dramatic "trust-busting." Circuit Judge William Howard Taft carefully distinguished the case of the Addyston Company and other pipe manufacturers from the sugar-trust case. In the present case, he explained, the facts were different.

These companies conspired to fix prices, said Taft, before they agreed with their customers in 36 states to deliver shipments of pipe; therefore they were within interstate commerce and the power of Congress. Price fixing restrained trade as surely as pipe contained oil, and Congress had passed the Anti-Trust Act to release trade. Free enterprise, Taft insisted, meant free competition.

When the Supreme Court affirmed Taft's ruling, other judges had a new precedent to follow and the Sherman Act a new vitality.

Energy personified, Theodore Roosevelt became President after William McKinley's assassination, and faced what he called the "absolutely vital question"—whether the United States Government had the power to control the giant corporations of the day.

Money personified, the magnificent J. P.

Morgan dominated finance, the Northern Pacific and other railroads, and the billion-dollar U. S. Steel Corporation; his ally James J. Hill had the Great Northern line. E. H. Harriman, with his Southern Pacific and Union Pacific routes and his friends in Standard Oil, had challenged Morgan and Hill for control of a railroad into Chicago.

After a fight that wrecked the stock market, the three agreed to combine forces. They organized a holding company, a New Jersey corporation called Northern Securities, and leaned back to enjoy their monopoly on transportation in the Northwest.

Roosevelt ordered the Attorney General to enforce the Sherman Act against them. In the Supreme Court their lawyers argued that only New Jersey could regulate a New Jersey corporation, that stock transactions were not within interstate commerce, that

having power did not amount to abusing it.

Justice Harlan read the Court's opinion in March, 1904, to a crowded courtroom and an anxious country. New Jersey did not have Congress at its mercy, he ruled; he called the point about stocks a mere straw man; and Congress, he said bluntly, meant to prevent the "mere existence" of such trusts. If the company was secure the Northwest was not: "the entire commerce of the immense . . . part of the United States between the Great Lakes and the Pacific at Puget Sound will be at the mercy of a single holding corporation. . . ." As the court below had ordered, the Northern Securities Company must be dissolved.

After this victory and others, the government attacked the Standard Oil empire. More than ten states had moved against it under their own antitrust laws by 1906, when federal attorneys filed suit under the Sherman Act. After 15 months of testimony that filled 21 printed volumes, federal judges in St. Louis ordered the oil trust broken up.

When the Supreme Court reviewed the case, it affirmed the order but altered the law. Congress, said Chief Justice Edward Douglass White, only meant the law to punish "unreasonable" restraint of trade. The "rule of reason" became a rule of law.

"UNREASONABLE, unnecessary and arbitrary," a violation of liberty under the Fourteenth Amendment—thus five members of the Supreme Court held a New York law unconstitutional. This law said bakers must not work more than 10 hours a day or 60 hours a week.

Joseph Lochner had a bakery in Utica, and New York fined him $20 for overworking Frank Couverette. For a second offense, he drew $50 in fines or 50 days in jail. His case reached the Court in 1905.

States, ruled Justice Rufus W. Peckham, must not pass such laws, "mere meddlesome interferences" to keep grown men from taking care of themselves. States have a "police power" to protect the public, but they may not limit such individual rights as liberty of contract: A worker must be free to make his own contract with his employer.

Justice Harlan dissented, citing evidence that bakers suffered eye and lung troubles, that New York might protect their health. And Oliver Wendell Holmes, who had joined the Court in 1902, dissented sepa-

"NEXT CAR!" a conductor directs a Negro family, motioning them to a "Colored Only" coach. Louisiana's Jim Crow Law forbade blacks to sit with whites on trains. Attorney Albion Tourgée (above) argued for Homer Adolph Plessy, a Negro who tested the law by entering a forbidden coach. But the Supreme Court's decision in **Plessy v. Ferguson** proved the temper of the 1890's: Races could be segregated if equal facilities were provided (left). For decades after this decision, its famous "separate but equal" doctrine remained a rule of law.

rately, to say that "a constitution is not intended to embody a particular economic theory," that laws might rest on "novel and even shocking" ideas and be constitutional.

Oregon had passed a law to keep women from working more than 10 hours a day in factories and laundries. Curt Muller, owner of a laundry in Portland, Oregon, was convicted of breaking it; he fought his conviction through state courts to the Supreme Court, relying on Peckham's opinion in *Lochner* v. *New York*. He also claimed that the Oregon statute could not meet the Constitution's demand for "due process of law."

Historically, that had meant "a fair trial." But judges were using it to protect property from laws they found unreasonable.

One reform group wanted the best possible lawyer for Oregon's case. Joseph H. Choate of New York turned it down; he didn't see why a "big husky Irishwoman should not work more than ten hours if she so desired." A famous corporation lawyer in Boston accepted—Louis D. Brandeis.

Studying Peckham's opinion in the Lochner case, Brandeis considered its reference to "common knowledge" that baking was a healthy trade. Boldly and shrewdly, he devoted only two pages of his brief to legal points; 100 cited facts from doctors, health officers, and factory inspectors to show that overworked women fell ill, turned to drink, bore sickly children and then neglected them.

No one had ever submitted such a brief to the Court. But the Justices accepted it, and praised him for it in their unani-

"**WHY NOT LET ME IN?**" *asks Cuba in a 1902 cartoon. "Puerto Rico is inside." Acquiring both islands from Spain in 1898, the United States gave sovereignty to Cuba. It kept Puerto Rico; the island's canefields (below) produced quarrels among sugar growers and a lawsuit over American tariff duties on foreign goods. When the Supreme Court reviewed this case in 1901, it held that tariffs did not apply to U.S. possessions. Such suits posed the question: How does the Constitution apply to unforeseen problems— does it follow the flag? In these "Insular Cases," the Court declared that the Constitution would protect liberty anywhere under the Stars and Stripes, and would give Congress power to govern the new "American empire."*

mous decision to uphold the law of Oregon.

"When an evil is a national evil, it must be cured by a national remedy," cried Senator Albert J. Beveridge of Indiana. Reformers were demanding change in politics, business, society in general; in response, Congress was assuming a "police power" for the whole country.

Disturbed by reports of filth in meatpacking plants, it passed pure food and drug laws. Shocked by stories of the "white slave trade," it passed the Mann Act. The Supreme Court upheld these laws, and others.

But when President Woodrow Wilson nominated Brandeis for Associate Justice in January, 1916, the *New York Times* thought the Court no place for "a striver after changes." William Howard Taft and Joseph H. Choate called him "not a fit person" for the bench. The Senate wrangled for almost five months before confirming him.

Of all challenges to reform, child labor was the most poignant; "a subject for the combined intelligence and massed morality of American people to handle," said Senator Beveridge. In 1916 Congress passed a law to keep goods made by child labor out of interstate commerce.

As a result, John Dagenhart, less than 14, would lose his job in a textile mill in Charlotte, North Carolina. His brother, Reuben, not yet 16, would lose 12 hours of piecework a week.

Their father asked the federal district court to enjoin the factory from obeying the law and United States Attorney William C. Hammer from enforcing it. As "a man of small means," with a large family, he com-

plained, he needed the boys' pay for their "comfortable support and maintenance." Their work was "altogether in the production of manufactured goods" and had "nothing whatsoever" to do with commerce.

When the district judge granted the injunctions, the U. S. attorney appealed to the Supreme Court. Five Justices thought that in enacting the Child Labor Law Congress had usurped the powers of the states; such laws might destroy the federal system.

Legislation can begin where an evil begins, retorted Justice Holmes, dissenting. If Congress chooses to prohibit trade in "the product of ruined lives," the Court should not outlaw its choice. He added: "I should have thought that if we were to introduce our own moral conceptions where in my opinion they do not belong, this was preëminently a case for upholding the exercise of all its powers by the United States."

Three Justices joined Holmes's dissent. So did Congress; it promptly set high taxes on products of child labor. But in 1922 the Court decided that this law imposed a penalty, not a tax, and held it invalid. Chief Justice William Howard Taft wrote an opinion saying the Tenth Amendment reserves problems like child labor for the states to solve.

Not until 1941 did the Court overrule its child labor decisions. Meanwhile, reformers urged an amendment to protect children, and called the Court a "Supreme Legislature." They pointed out: "The vote of one member of the Supreme Court may exceed the collective power of 435 Representatives and ninety-six Senators, or even of 100,000,000 people."

Two months after Congress declared war on Germany in April, 1917, it passed an Espionage Act that punished attempts to obstruct enlistment and discipline in the armed forces. In 1918 it passed a Sedition Act so broadly worded that almost any critical comment on the war or the government might incur a fine of $10,000, or 20 years in prison, or both.

Under the 1917 law, government attorneys filed almost 2,000 prosecutions, among them *United States* v. *"The Spirit of '76."* Only a handful of these cases reached the Supreme Court. Only after the Armistice did the Justices hear a case challenging the law by the First Amendment guarantee of free speech.

Charles T. Schenck and other members of the Socialist Party in Philadelphia were convicted of conspiring to mail circulars to drafted men. In forbidding slavery, these leaflets said, the Thirteenth Amendment forbade the draft.

For a unanimous Court, Holmes wrote that "in many places and in ordinary times" the Socialists would be within their constitutional rights. But the Bill of Rights does not protect words creating a "clear and pres-ent danger" of "evils that Congress has a right to prevent." Schenck was sentenced to six months in jail.

But Holmes and Brandeis dissented when the 1918 Sedition Act, and leaflets in English and Yiddish, came before them. Flung from a factory window to the New York streets on August 23, 1918, these papers summoned "the workers of the world" to defend the Russian Revolution against despots. "P.S.," said some, "We hate and despise German militarism more than do your hypocritical tyrants." By a seven-to-two majority, the Court upheld criminal convictions under the Act.

In his eloquent dissent, Holmes remarked, "Congress certainly cannot forbid all effort to change the mind of the country." He saw no national danger in the "usual tall talk" of "these poor and puny anonymities." But he saw danger in persecution of opinions, for "time has upset many fighting faiths" and the national good requires "free trade in ideas." To reach the truth, people must weigh many opinions.

"That at any rate is the theory of our Constitution. It is an experiment, as all life is an experiment," Justice Holmes concluded.

"TRUST-BUSTER" *Theodore Roosevelt defies the goliaths of Wall Street. James J. Hill and J. P. Morgan, through a stock monopoly called Northern Securities, controlled railroads in the northwestern states; President Roosevelt ordered a suit against them under the Sherman Anti-Trust Act. In 1904 the Supreme Court affirmed a lower court's judgment breaking up the monopoly. This decision (**Northern Securities v. U. S.**) was hailed as a victory for the public interest over the trusts.*

FRENZIED SELLING *racks the stock market in the panic of 1901 when Morgan, Hill, and E. H. Harriman fought to a stalemate for control of railroad shares. Finally agreeing on a compromise, the three formed the Northern Securities Company.*

ONE OF THE GREAT DISSENTERS,
*John Marshall Harlan won fame as
a defender of democracy during 33
years as an Associate Justice, serving
from 1877 to 1911.*

*He protested sharply in the Standard
Oil case, when the Court said that no
companies may "unreasonably"
restrain trade. The Sherman Act
forbids "every" trust or combination
in restraint of interstate commerce;
Harlan thundered, "The Court has now
read into the Act of Congress words
which are not to be found there."*

*Onetime Kentucky slaveholder,
Harlan fought for the Union in the
Civil War. Appointed to the Supreme
Court by President Rutherford B.
Hayes, he carried on an ardent
battle for civil rights.*

*Dissenting in Plessy v. Ferguson, he
wrote: ". . . in view of the Constitution,
in the eye of the law, there is in this
country no superior, dominant, ruling
class of citizens. . . . The humblest is
the peer of the most powerful."*

*Good-humored and convivial, he
limited his disagreements to the
conference room, and enjoyed whist
parties with fellow Justices. Oliver
Wendell Holmes called him "the last
of the tobacco-spittin' judges." A
friend said that Harlan retired at night
"with one hand on the Constitution
and the other on the Bible."*

THE OCTOPUS: *Standard Oil, first of the
great American trusts, came to symbolize
wealth and power running wild, crushing*

"Any agitator who read these thirty-four
pages to a mob would not stir them to violence, except possibly against himself,"
decided one reader of Benjamin Gitlow's
"Left Wing Manifesto." But when that
pamphlet appeared in 1919, New York authorities arrested Gitlow under the state's
criminal anarchy law.

Gitlow applied to the Supreme Court.
Seven Justices upheld his conviction and
the New York statute. But they assumed—
for the first time—that freedom of speech
and of the press, which the First Amendment protects from any Act of Congress,
are among the rights which the Fourteenth

industry and government alike, as this 1904 cartoon indicates. When the Supreme Court held in 1911 that the oil monopoly must be broken up for the sake of restoring free competition, the ruling won widespread acclaim as a victory for the public.

Amendment forbids any state to abridge.

Holmes and Brandeis would have set Gitlow free. As Holmes explained, they did not think his "redundant discourse" a public danger. The majority called it "a direct incitement." Holmes replied calmly: "Every idea is an incitement."

Gitlow served three years in Sing Sing prison. Later he became one of the Communist Party's bitterest critics.

In 1925, while the Court was deciding Gitlow's case, Minnesota legislators were passing a new statute. It provided that a court order could silence, as "public nuisances," periodicals that published "malicious, scandalous, and defamatory" material.

"Unfortunately we are both former editors of a local scandal sheet, a distinction we regret," conceded J. M. Near and his partner in the first issue of the *Saturday Press,* but they promised to fight crime in Minneapolis. They called the police chief a "cuddler of criminals" who protected "rat gamblers." They abused the county attorney, who sued Near; the state's highest court ordered the paper suppressed. Citing the *Schenck* and *Gitlow* decisions, Near's lawyer appealed to the Supreme Court, which struck down the state law.

For four dissenters, Pierce Butler quoted

69

CONTROVERSIAL CONFECTIONERY: *Joseph Lochner's Home Bakery in Utica, New York, made legal history in a 1905 Supreme Court case involving working hours. His son, Joseph Lochner, Jr., stands in the bakery's doorway (below) with his mother, left, and a niece. In a damaged interior view (above), they pose with employees. Joseph Lochner, Jr., granted permission to publish these family photographs taken in 1908.*

BAKERY OWNER JOSEPH LOCHNER (*second from right*) *fought charges that he broke a New York maximum-hour statute. The Supreme Court struck down the law (**Lochner v. New York**), ruling that the Fourteenth Amendment protects "liberty of contract" between workers and employers.*

with evident distaste Near's outbursts at "snake-faced" Jewish gangsters; peace and order need legal protection from such publishers, Butler insisted.

For the majority, Chief Justice Charles Evans Hughes analyzed this "unusual, if not unique" law. If anyone published something "scandalous" a Minnesota court might close his paper permanently for damaging public morals. But charges of corruption in office always make public scandals, Hughes pointed out. Anyone defamed in print may sue for libel, he added emphatically.

However disgusting Near's words, said Hughes, the words of the Constitution controlled the decision, and they demand a free press without censorship. Criticism may offend public officials, it may even remove them from office; but trashy or trenchant, the press may not be suppressed by law.

How citizens use liberty has confronted the Justices again and again, in cases of violence as well as scandal.

Frank Moore faced an Arkansas electric chair; so did Ed Hicks, J. E. Knox, Ed Coleman, and Paul Hall. All five were Negroes. When a federal district court said that it could not help them, they took their petition for a writ of habeas corpus to the Supreme Court, and raised the question: How does the Constitution protect the right to a fair trial in state courts?

Announcing the ruling of the Court, Justice Holmes gave their story as it appeared from the trial record and the sworn statements of other witnesses:

Black sharecroppers in the cotton country around Elaine, Arkansas, decided that their landlords oppressed and cheated them. On the night of September 30, 1919, they

PHILOSOPHIC DISSENTER, *Oliver Wendell Holmes, a dashing figure who spoke with the eloquence of a romantic, created new concepts in judicial thinking. As a Justice he inspired generations of lawyers to shun classic attitudes of jurisprudence and recognize that law changes with society's needs. Highly sophisticated, Holmes approached law with a skeptical and objective mind.*

*Chosen for the Court by President Theodore Roosevelt in 1902, Holmes boldly accused his associates of reading into the Constitution economic rather than legal theories. When the Court killed a state law that set maximum hours for bakers (*Lochner v. New York*), he wrote one of the most famous dissents in history: ". . . a constitution is not intended to embody a particular economic theory. . . . It is made for people of fundamentally differing views. . . ."*

Holmes's life spanned almost 94 years. Wounded three times in the Civil War, he lived to serve the law until 1935. Appointed a Justice at 61, he worked in a world of ideas and values, and took pleasure "just in trying to exhibit some hint of horizons." Master of his profession, he retired from the Court at age 90.

met in the Hoop Spur church to plan ways of getting help from a lawyer. Armed white men attacked them; in the fight that followed, one white man was killed.

News and rumors spread; armed posses hurried to Elaine. Blacks were hunted down and shot, even women working in the cotton fields. On October 1, Clinton Lee, a white man, was killed; Moore, Hicks, Knox, Coleman, and Hall were arrested for murder.

The Governor asked the Army to restore order, and named a Committee of Seven to investigate the riots. When a lynch mob surrounded the jail, soldiers stood guard while the committee promised that the law would execute the five murderers. The mob waited to see what would happen.

Two white men and several blacks swore later that the committee tortured blacks until they agreed to testify against the prisoners. Indicted by a white grand jury for first-degree murder, the defendants faced a white trial jury on November 3; a threatening crowd filled the courthouse and the streets outside. In 45 minutes the trial was over; in two or three minutes the jury gave its verdict: "Guilty."

From the affidavits presented to the Court, Holmes concluded, "if any prisoner by any chance had been acquitted by a jury he could not have escaped the mob."

All appeals in the state courts had failed.

Normally, federal courts will not interfere with the courts of any state on matters of state law. But, warned Holmes, if "the whole proceeding is a mask"—if "an irresistible wave of public passion" sweeps the prisoners through the courts "to the fatal end"—then nothing can prevent the Supreme Court "from securing to the petitioners their constitutional rights."

The district judge should have examined the facts for himself, Holmes ruled, to see if the story in Moore's petition was true and if the state had not given its prisoners a fair trial. *Moore* v. *Dempsey* went back for the district judge to hear.

Eventually, all five defendants went free; so did nearly a hundred other blacks arrested during the riots. Federal judges had a new precedent, citizens a new safeguard. Justice may wear a blindfold, ruled the Supreme Court, but not a mask.

Alabama militia had machine guns on the courthouse roof, said newspaper reports from Scottsboro; mobs had a band playing "There'll Be a Hot Time in the Old Town Tonight"; and amid the clamor, nine black youths waited behind bars for trial on charges of raping two white women.

Victoria Price and Ruby Bates, two white mill workers, were riding a slow freight from Chattanooga on their way home to Huntsville on March 25, 1931. Across the Alabama line, white and black hoboes on board got into a fight; some jumped and some were thrown from the train. Alerted by telephone, a sheriff's posse stopped the train, arrested the nine Negroes still on it, and took them to jail in the Jackson County seat, Scottsboro. Then Victoria Price claimed they had raped her and Ruby Bates.

Doctors found no proof of this story, but a frenzied crowd gathered swiftly. Ten thousand people, many armed, were there a week later when the nine went on trial.

OVERWORKED LAUNDRESS *in the shop of Curt Muller (above, arms folded) led to a Court ruling: States may enforce maximum hours for women (**Muller v. Oregon**). Lawyer Louis D. Brandeis (below) revolutionized legal briefs by using medical and sociological facts to show evils of unregulated working conditions.*

"**THE NEW HAND.**" *Young, wide-eyed girl reports for her first day at a textile mill in this cartoon—one of many attacks on the "national evil" of child labor in the early 1900's. Workers often developed tuberculosis in the warm, moist air of poorly ventilated spinning rooms such as the one shown below.*

Because state law provided a death penalty, it required the court to appoint one or two defense lawyers. At the arraignment, the judge told all seven members of the county bar to serve. Six made excuses.

In three trials, completed in three days, jurors found eight defendants guilty; they could not agree on Roy Wright, one of the youngest. The eight were sentenced to death.

Of these nine, the oldest might have reached 21; one was crippled, one nearly blind; each signed his name by "X"—"his mark." All swore they were innocent.

On appeal, Alabama's highest court ordered a new hearing for one of the nine, Eugene Williams; but it upheld the other proceedings.

When a petition in the name of Ozie Powell reached the Supreme Court, seven Justices agreed that no lawyer had helped the defendants at the trials. Justice George Sutherland wrote the Court's opinion. Facing a possible death sentence, unable to hire a lawyer, too young or ignorant or dull to defend himself—such a defendant has a constitutional right to counsel, and his counsel must fight for him, Sutherland said.

Sent back for retrial, the cases went on. *Norris* v. *Alabama* reached the Supreme Court in 1935; Chief Justice Hughes ruled that because qualified Negroes did not serve on jury duty in those counties, the trials had been unconstitutional.

"We still have the right to secede!" retorted one southern official. Again the prisoners stood trial. Alabama dropped rape charges against some; others were convicted but later paroled; one escaped.

The Supreme Court's rulings stood —if a defendant lacks a lawyer and a fairly chosen jury, the Constitution can help him.

And the Constitution forbids any state's prosecuting attorneys to use evidence they know is false; the Court announced this in 1935, when

BROWN BROTHERS (ABOVE) AND LEWIS HINE COLLECTION, LIBRARY OF CONGRESS

CHOKING DUST *congests the lungs of boys picking slate from coal in a Pennsylvania mine. Below, a Louisiana cannery breaks state law by employing children to shuck oysters. For their work, youngsters usually got only a few cents a day. In 1918 and 1922 the Supreme Court held invalid federal laws against child labor; it overruled these decisions in 1941.*

FILM EPIC *or espionage? The case of* The Spirit of '76 *arose like almost 2,000 others when the 1917 Espionage Act endangered freedom of speech during the feverish days of World War I. Poster at right announces the premiere of '76 in Los Angeles. The 12-reel photoplay portrayed events of the American Revolution— clashes between patriots and English and signing of the Declaration of Independence.*

Federal prosecutors charged that the film's producer, Robert Goldstein, a suspected German sympathizer, tried to arouse hatred between America and her World War I ally, England, by inserting scenes showing British soldiers committing atrocities in the Revolutionary War. Officials seized the film and Goldstein was convicted (**United States v. "The Spirit of '76"**).

Under a new law, the 1918 Sedition Act, similar cases in the lower courts further threatened freedom of speech. Only after the Armistice did the Supreme Court review a scant number of these cases; Goldstein's was not among them. His movie script survives in the Library of Congress. But the film is lost. Weeks of intensive search uncovered these rare photographs made during the filming and owned by Charles E. Toberman, a Los Angeles resident, who invested money in the 1917 extravaganza.

that gave each circuit a court of appeals with power to make a final decision in a great many cases. This law also ended the Justices' trips on circuit duty. Before long the Supreme Court was keeping up with its schedules. But as new laws regulated business and working conditions, and suits challenging these laws reached the courts, overloaded dockets plagued the Justices again.

After Chief Justice Fuller's death in 1910, President Taft broke tradition by choosing an Associate Justice, Edward Douglass White, for Chief.

When White died in 1921, President Harding made Taft Chief Justice, the only former Chief Executive ever to hold the highest judicial office. Taft was vastly delighted, for the Chief Justiceship, not the Presidency, had always been the honor he wanted most.

Considering the clogged machinery of the federal courts, where the caseload was rising again, Taft remarked: "A rich man can stand the delay... but the poor man always suffers." The new Chief Justice set out to improve the whole federal judiciary.

He planned the Conference of Senior Circuit Court Judges, a source of many reforms in judicial practice. The law establishing the conference permitted judges of one area to help elsewhere on courts swamped with work. Then Taft broke tradition to lobby for the "Judges' Bill," passed in 1925.

By limiting the right of appeal, this law let the Supreme Court devote its attention to constitutional issues and important questions of federal law. In most cases since 1925, the parties ask permission to be heard; the Justices grant or deny it at discretion.

Before gaining freedom to choose cases, the Court surprised many observers in 1923 by a choice of precedents to decide *Adkins* v. *Children's Hospital*. In the majority opinion, Justice Sutherland returned to the "meddlesome interferences" doctrine of *Lochner* v. *New York,* the bakery case of 1905.

Congress had passed a law to guarantee minimum wages for women and children

Tom Mooney had spent nearly 20 years behind the bars of a California prison.

To rally support for a stronger Army and Navy, San Franciscans organized a huge parade for "Preparedness Day," July 22, 1916. As the marchers set out, a bomb exploded; 10 victims died, 40 were injured. Mooney, known as a friend of anarchists and a labor radical, was convicted of first-degree murder; soon it appeared that the chief witness against him had lied under oath. President Wilson persuaded the Governor of California to commute the death sentence to life imprisonment. For years labor called Mooney a martyr to injustice.

Finally Mooney's lawyers applied to the Supreme Court for a writ of habeas corpus, and won a new ruling—if a state uses perjured witnesses, knowing that they lie, it violates the Fourteenth Amendment's guarantee of due process of law; it must provide ways to set aside such tainted convictions. The case went back to the state. In 1939 Governor Culbert Olson granted Mooney a pardon; free, he was almost forgotten.

"JUSTICE DELAYED is justice denied" —the Supreme Court saw this in 1887, when it was almost four years behind in its work. Appealing to the public, Chief Justice Waite sought "relief for the people against the tedious and oppressive delays" of federal justice. In 1891 Congress passed a law

EUGENE V. DEBS (*speaking above*) *fought for workers' rights. For his role in the 1894 Pullman strike, he went to jail. Labor bitterly attacked the Supreme Court for letting his sentence stand.*

BEHIND BARS *on a sedition charge, Socialist Debs wins Presidential nomination in 1920. He lost to Warren Harding, who set him free.*

working in the District of Columbia. A children's hospital attacked the law; the case reached the Supreme Court. Five Justices agreed that the law violated the due process clause of the Fifth Amendment and the right to liberty of contract. Sutherland hinted that since women had won the right to vote they were legally equal to men, so Congress should not single them out for special protection.

"It will need more than the Nineteenth Amendment to convince me that there are no differences between men and women," Holmes retorted, dissenting, "or that legislation cannot take those differences into account." On the "dogma" of liberty of contract, he remarked: "pretty much all law consists in forbidding men to do some things that they want to do, and contract is no more exempt from law than other acts."

Taft also dissented. He had always supposed, he said, that *Lochner* had been overruled by later decisions; and, he added, poor workers cannot meet an employer on an equal level of choice.

But Arizona, Arkansas, and New York saw their minimum-wage laws go down under the *Adkins* precedent.

Justice Sutherland always believed that judges were the best guardians of liberty. Chosen for learning, ability, and impartiality, judges were safer guides than any other men. Courts were wiser than crowds.

"I am an optimist in all things," Sutherland said once. He felt sure that evolution's universal laws were making the world better and that meddlesome legislation could only bring trouble. Often he spoke for the famous "four horsemen"—himself, Pierce Butler, James C. McReynolds, and Willis Van Devanter. Joined by one other Justice, they could say what laws were valid.

By 1930 Harvard Professor Felix Frankfurter took stock: "Since 1920 the Court has invalidated more legislation than in fifty years preceding." When Taft retired that year, President Hoover wanted Charles Evans Hughes for Chief Justice. Debating the appointment, one Senator accused the Justices of "fixing policies for the people . . . when they should leave that to Congress," another called the Court "the economic dictator in the United States." But the Senate

COMMUNIST CANDIDATES, *William Z. Foster (left) and his running mate Benjamin Gitlow lost miserably in the 1928 Presidential race. In 1925 the Supreme Court had upheld a New York conviction of Gitlow for publishing the "Left Wing Manifesto." This ponderous article, calling workers to rise against capitalism, appeared in* The Revolutionary Age *(above).*

confirmed Hughes for Chief, and Owen J. Roberts for Associate a few months later.

Nicknamed the "roving Justices," Hughes and Roberts sometimes joined the "four horsemen," sometimes joined three Judges more willing to accept laws however meddlesome. These three were Brandeis, Harlan Fiske Stone, and Holmes until he retired in 1932. Benjamin N. Cardozo succeeded him, and often voted with Brandeis and Stone.

WHEN THE STOCK MARKET collapsed in 1929 and the American economy headed toward ruin, President Hoover called for emergency measures. The states tried to cope with the general disaster. Before long, cases on their new laws began to reach the Supreme Court. Franklin D. Roosevelt won the 1932 Presidential election, and by June, 1933, Congress had passed 15 major laws for national remedies.

Almost 20,000,000 people depended on federal relief by 1934, when the Supreme Court decided the case of Leo Nebbia. New York's milk-control board had fixed the lawful price of milk at nine cents a quart; the state had convicted Nebbia, a Rochester grocer, of selling two quarts and a five-cent loaf of bread for only 18 cents. Nebbia had appealed. Justice Roberts wrote the majority opinion, upholding the New York law; he went beyond the 1887 decision in the Granger cases to declare that a state may regulate any business whatever when the public good requires it. The "four horsemen" dissented; but Roosevelt's New Dealers began to hope their economic program might win the Supreme Court's approval after all.

They were wrong. Considering a New Deal law for the first time, in January, 1935, the Court held that one part of the National Industrial Recovery Act gave the President too much lawmaking power.

The Court did sustain the policy of reducing the dollar's value in gold. But a five-to-four decision in May made a railroad pen-

U. S. ARMY TROOPS *guard Negroes rounded up near Elaine, Arkansas, after racial violence broke out in the autumn of 1919. Black sharecroppers had felt white landlords were cheating them. Local authorities feared subsequent riots were the beginning of a mass-murder plot.*

sion law unconstitutional. Then all nine Justices vetoed a law to relieve farm debtors, and killed the National Recovery Administration; FDR denounced their "horse-and-buggy" definition of interstate commerce.

While the Court moved into its splendid new building, criticism of its decisions grew sharper and angrier. The whole federal judiciary came under attack as district courts issued—over a two-year period—some 1,600 injunctions to keep Acts of Congress from being enforced. But the Court seemed to ignore the clamor.

Farming lay outside Congressional power, said six Justices in 1936; they called the Agricultural Adjustment Act invalid for dealing with state problems. Brandeis and Cardozo joined Stone in a scathing dissent: "Courts are not the only agency . . . that must be assumed to have capacity to govern." But two decisions that followed denied power to both the federal and the state governments.

In a law to strengthen the chaotic soft-coal industry and help the almost starving miners, Congress had

SCENE OF VIOLENCE: *Black sharecroppers air grievances in Hoop Spur church near Elaine. White men park nearby. Suddenly gunfire explodes into the "Elaine Massacre." Frank Moore and other blacks were sentenced to die for murder. The Supreme Court considered their claim that mob domination barred fair trial, and returned the case to a federal court for investigation (**Moore** v. **Dempsey**). Eventually, all defendants went free.*

81

dealt with prices in one section, with working conditions and wages in another. If the courts held one section invalid, the other might survive. When a test case came up, seven coal-mining states urged the Court to uphold the Act, but five Justices called the whole law unconstitutional for trying to cure "local evils"—state problems.

Then they threw out a New York law that set minimum wages for women and children; they said states could not regulate matters of individual liberty.

By forbidding Congress and the states to act, Stone confided bitterly to his sister, the Court had apparently "tied Uncle Sam up in a hard knot."

That November Roosevelt won reelection by a margin of ten million votes; Democrats won more than three-fourths of the seats in Congress. The people had spoken. Yet the laws their representatives passed might stand or fall by five or six votes in the Supreme Court. Roosevelt, aware that Congress had changed the number of Justices six times since 1789, sent a plan for court reform to the Senate on February 5, 1937.

Emphasizing the limited vision of "older men," Roosevelt asked Congress for power to name an additional Justice when one aged 70 did not resign, until the Court should have 15 members. (Six were already over 70; Brandeis was 80.) Roosevelt said the Court needed help to keep up with its work.

Even staunch New Dealers boggled at this plan; it incurred criticism as sharp as any the Court had ever provoked. Chief Justice Hughes calmly pointed out that the Court was keeping up with its work. And in angry editorials and thousands of letters to Congress the public protested the very idea of "packing" the Court.

Before the President revealed his plan, five Justices had already voted to sustain a state minimum-wage law in a case from Washington; on March 29, the Court announced that the law was constitutional.

On April 12, Chief Justice Hughes read the majority opinion in *National Labor Relations Board* v. *Jones & Laughlin Steel Corporation*. It upheld the Wagner Act, the first federal law to regulate disputes between capital and labor. Hughes gave interstate commerce a definition broader than the Jones & Laughlin domain—mines in Minnesota, quarries in West Virginia, steamships on the Great Lakes. Although the case

turned on a union dispute at one plant in Pennsylvania, he said, a company-wide dispute would paralyze interstate commerce. Congress could prevent such evils and protect union rights.

Under these two rulings, Congress and the states were free to exercise powers the Court had denied just a year before. Stubbornly the "four horsemen" dissented. But Van Devanter announced that he would retire. By autumn the fight over the Court was a thing of the past.

As Lincoln said in 1861, the people would rule themselves; they would decide vital questions of national policy. But, as firmly as Lincoln himself, they disclaimed "any assault upon the Court." In one of the Supreme Court's greatest crises, the people chose to sustain its power and dignity.

DECISIONS CHANGED dramatically in the "constitutional revolution" of 1937. So did the Court when President Roosevelt made appointments at last.

In 1937 he named Senator Hugo L. Black; in 1938, Solicitor General Stanley Reed; in 1939, Felix Frankfurter and William O. Douglas, Chairman of the Securities and Exchange Commission. Attorney General Frank Murphy came to the bench in 1940; Senator James F. Byrnes of South Carolina, in 1941.

When Hughes retired that year, Roosevelt made Stone Chief Justice and gave his seat as Associate to Attorney General Robert H. Jackson. How the "new Court" would meet old problems soon became clear.

Congress passed the Fair Labor Standards Act in 1938. It banned child labor, regulated hours, and set minimum wages—25 cents an hour—in interstate commerce. *United States* v. *Darby Lumber Co.* brought the law before the Court in 1941.

If the Justices followed the child-labor decisions of 1918 and 1922, they would veto the law; but all nine called it valid.

But new problems tested the Court as it was defining civil liberties. Danger from abroad made the case for patriotism and freedom in America more urgent; in the "blood purge" of 1934, Adolf Hitler had announced, "I became the supreme judge of the German people."

Under God's law, the Commandments in the Book of Exodus, members of Jehovah's Witnesses refuse to salute a flag.

JUDICIAL ARCHITECT, *William Howard Taft, tenth Chief Justice, streamlined the Nation's system of legal review. At his persuasion, Congress passed the "Judges' Bill" in 1925. This stripped the Supreme Court of routine cases, leaving Justices free to hear only suits that involved major constitutional questions and problems of federal law.*

He won another victory when Congress provided funds for the first Supreme Court Building. With the Justices in 1929 (left), Taft studies architect Cass Gilbert's model. When the cornerstone was laid in 1932, Chief Justice Charles Evans Hughes said of Taft, who had died two years before: "This building is the result of his intelligent persistence."

Taft realized a lifelong ambition when President Harding appointed him Chief Justice in 1921. Taft later wrote, "...the court...next to my wife and children, is the nearest thing to my heart in life." Before becoming Chief Justice, he served as the twenty-seventh President—the only man to hold both offices.

HEAVILY GUARDED *by armed state militia, black youths walk toward the Jackson County courthouse at Scottsboro, Alabama. Charged with assaulting two white women, the defendants stood their first trial in 1931 when 19-year-old Ruby Bates (left, on witness stand) said the Negroes had attacked her and a friend. At a later trial in 1933 she swore that her original story was a lie, but her repentant testimony failed to convince the jury. She later led a demonstration to the White House in an appeal for the freedom of the nine Negroes.*

When Lillian and William Gobitas (misspelled "Gobitis" in the record), aged 12 and 10 in 1935, refused to join classmates in saluting the Stars and Stripes, the Board of Education in Minersville, Pennsylvania, decided to expel them for "insubordination." With help from other Witnesses and the American Civil Liberties Union, their father sought relief in the federal courts. The district court and the circuit court of appeals granted it. In 1940 the school board turned to the Supreme Court.

Considering the right of local authorities to settle local problems, eight Justices voted to uphold the school board's "secular regulation." Justice Frankfurter wrote the majority opinion. He told Justice Stone that his private idea "of liberty and toleration and good sense" favored the Gobitas family, but he believed that judges should defer to the actions of the people's elected representatives.

Hitler's armies had stabbed into France when Frankfurter announced the Court's ruling on June 3, 1940; Stone read his dissent with obvious emotion, insisting that the Constitution must preserve "freedom of mind and spirit."

Law reviews criticized the Court for setting aside the issue of religious freedom. Jehovah's Witnesses suffered violent attacks around the country; many states expelled children from school for not saluting the flag.

"SCOTTSBORO BOYS" *confer with lawyer Sam Leibowitz, who later became a famous New York judge. His masterly defense focused world attention on the Alabama trials where eight of the defendants were convicted and sentenced to death in the electric chair. The spotlight of the Scottsboro cases fell on Haywood Patterson (seated). When Leibowitz and his co-counsel showed that qualified Negroes had been barred from jury duty, and claimed that the youths had been denied a fair trial, the Supreme Court reversed their convictions. Alabama tried them again. In an Alabama courtroom with Leibowitz (opposite), Patterson holds a horseshoe for good luck. It failed him. He was four times tried and convicted of attacking the two white women.*

West Virginia law required all schools to teach "Americanism," and in 1942 the State Board of Education ordered all teachers and pupils to salute the flag. A child who refused might be punished as a "delinquent," his parents might be fined or jailed.

Walter Barnette and other Witnesses with school-age children sued for a federal injunction against these penalties; in 1943 the Supreme Court heard the case argued.

On Flag Day, June 14, the Court flatly overruled and repudiated the *Gobitis* decision. For the majority, Justice Jackson rejected the idea that a child's forced salute would foster national unity. He singled out as a "fixed star in our constitutional constellation" this fact—"no official, high or petty," can prescribe orthodoxy in politics, nationalism, or religion, for any citizen.

Justice Frankfurter still upheld the state's action against his own "purely personal" view, saying: "One who belongs to the most vilified and persecuted minority in history is not likely to be insensible to the freedoms guaranteed by our Constitution."

AGITATOR AND MARTYR *for labor, Tom Mooney, leaves San Quentin in 1939. Charged with murder for deaths in a 1916 Preparedness Day bombing, he escaped the gallows when facts indicated he had been convicted on perjured testimony. In 1918 the Governor of California commuted his sentence to life in prison; 20 years later, he was pardoned.*

"In this solemn hour we pledge our fullest cooperation to you, Mr. President, and to our country," said a telegram to President Roosevelt, December 7, 1941, from the Japanese American Citizens League, at news of the Japanese attack on Pearl Harbor.

By the spring of 1942 such citizens were a vilified minority in their own country. In February the President signed Executive Order 9066, authorizing the War Department to remove "any and all persons" from military areas it might name; Congress approved in a law passed March 21. The Western Defense Command ordered everyone of Japanese ancestry to stay indoors from 8 p.m. to 6 a.m. In May the Army ordered such persons to report for evacuation to "relocation centers"—detention camps.

Gordon K. Hirabayashi, a senior at the University of Washington, thought it was his duty as a citizen to disobey both these orders, to defend his constitutional rights. Convicted and sentenced to three months in prison, he applied to the Supreme Court.

Chief Justice Stone spoke for all nine in June, 1943: the curfew was within the war power of the President and Congress. Concurring, Douglas wrote that the Court did not consider the wisdom of the order; Murphy insisted that the government could take such measures only in "great emergency."

In *Korematsu* v. *United States,* argued in October and decided on December 18, 1944, the Court upheld an Army order banishing civilians of Japanese ancestry from the west coast—adults, foster children in white homes, citizens "with as little as one-sixteenth Japanese blood." Justice Black wrote the majority opinion, mentioning Toyosaburo Korematsu's unquestioned loyalty. Orders affecting one racial group are "immediately suspect," said Black, but the Court would accept the order "as of the time it was made," under the war power.

Three Justices dissented, calling the order "a clear violation of Constitutional rights," "utterly revolting among a free people."

That same day, the Court unanimously ordered the Central Utah Relocation Center to release Miss Mitsuye Endo. The War Relocation Authority had conceded she was a loyal, law-abiding citizen, but it had not allowed her to leave the center freely.

WIDE WORLD

TERRORIST BOMBING: *During Preparedness Day parade in San Francisco, spectators and marchers fell when a bomb exploded just off Market Street (above). Mooney claimed he was the man on the parapet at right, more than a mile from the disaster. Convicted nevertheless, he applied to the Supreme Court (**Mooney v. Holohan**). It ruled that the Constitution forbids use in state courts of testimony known to be perjury.*

NATIONAL GEOGRAPHIC PHOTOGRAPHER THOMAS NEBBIA © N.G.S.

Justice Douglas's opinion warned that power to defend the community is not power to detain trustworthy citizens. Federal courts may issue writs of habeas corpus in such cases, he said. "Loyalty is a matter of the heart and mind," added Douglas, "not of race, creed, or color."

AS DEFENSE COUNSEL for Richard Quirin and seven other prisoners, Col. Kenneth C. Royall and Col. Cassius M. Dowell decided that to obey one order of their Commander-in-Chief they had to defy another. Their clients, all German-born, had lived in America but returned before Pearl Harbor to study sabotage techniques at a school near Berlin.

In dense midnight fog on June 12, 1942, a German submarine edged toward Amagansett Beach, Long Island, to land Quirin and three comrades, in German uniform, in a rubber boat. On the beach they met an unarmed Coast Guardsman who pretended to believe their story about fishing, then went off to get help. Armed, his patrol hurried back—to hear U-boat diesels offshore, to dig up cases of TNT and bombs disguised

as pen-and-pencil sets, to notify the police and the Federal Bureau of Investigation.

Five nights later, Herbert Haupt, Werner Thiel, Edward Kerling, and Hermann Neubauer landed safely at Ponte Vedra Beach, Florida, from another U-boat. None of the saboteurs was successful. On June 27, the FBI announced the arrest of all eight.

President Roosevelt appointed a military commission to try them as spies under the Articles of War; and Colonels Royall and Dowell to defend them. He issued a proclamation closing all civilian courts to such enemies, but the defense decided, in duty to their clients, to disobey this. Challenging the commission's legal authority, they sought writs of habeas corpus from the Court.

After two days of hearing and questioning lawyers for both sides, the Court said that Congress, in the Articles of War, had provided for commissions to try such cases; that the President had lawfully appointed one; that the writs would not issue.

But in finding for the President, the Supreme Court set another precedent—a proclamation from the White House could not close the doors of the Court. An executive

STILL SMILING *31 years later, Leo Nebbia, former grocer of Rochester, New York, holds two bottles of milk, which by 1965 had more than tripled in price since he sold it for less than nine cents a quart during the Great Depression. He sought review in the Supreme Court after being convicted of breaking a state minimum-price law passed to protect the New York milk industry in the face of damaging price wars. Precedents from the 1920's suggested that the Court would strike down the law.*

*But in 1934 five Justices voted to sustain it as a reasonable measure to promote the public welfare (**Nebbia** v. **New York**). Nebbia paid a five-dollar fine.*

The picture at right appeared in a newspaper reporting the outcome of his case. For the picture opposite, Nebbia—in 1965 a realtor in Las Vegas—made a special journey to Rochester. He posed in his son's store, four times as large as the old one but at the same location. He died in June, 1974.

order would not annul its power to review government actions under law.

The President announced on August 8 that all the saboteurs had been convicted, six executed. Two who had cooperated with the FBI went to prison at hard labor.

Bridges and aluminum plants survived the saboteurs' visit unharmed; a friend and a father did not. From Werner Thiel's days in New York before his arrest, when he was watched by the FBI, came *Cramer* v. *United States*. For the first time the Supreme Court reviewed a conviction for treason; a five-to-four vote decided that the conviction could not stand.

Justice Jackson, for the majority, explained why. The Constitution outlines the law of a most intricate crime in two sentences "packed with controversy and difficulty," he said. Treason against the United States lies "only in levying War against them, or in adhering to their Enemies, giving them Aid and Comfort." Unless a person confesses "in open Court" or two witnesses testify "to the same overt Act" of treason, he cannot be found guilty.

The jury that convicted Anthony Cramer, a naturalized citizen, heard how he met two of the saboteurs, Thiel and Kerling, "enemies of the United States," at an inn and a cafeteria. Two witnesses swore that they drank and talked "long and earnestly." But no one proved what they said.

The jury had no evidence that Cramer gave the enemies shelter or advice "or even paid for their drinks." Before the war, Thiel and Cramer had shared "a small and luckless delicatessen enterprise." If they met in public "to tipple and trifle" this did not prove Cramer's treason in law.

Acts innocent by nature may serve a treasonous plan, Justice Douglas insisted for the four dissenters.

Another jury considered this point when Hans Max Haupt, a naturalized citizen, stood trial for treason. His son Herbert, one of the saboteurs, had already been executed. Witnesses swore that he had sheltered his son for six days in his Chicago apartment; he had helped him buy a car; he had helped him try to get back a job at a plant making lenses for the secret Norden bombsight. All these actions were harmless, even if proved, Haupt's lawyers argued.

UNFURLED "BLUE EAGLE," *symbol of the National Recovery Administration (NRA), rises above a delegation (left) headed by New York City's Mayor Fiorello H. La Guardia, in center foreground. President Franklin D. Roosevelt set up the NRA in 1933 under one of the most sweeping laws ever passed by Congress to regulate commerce among the states.*

As an emergency measure, the NRA attempted, through federal control, to promote the recovery of the Nation's industry, create work for the mass of Great Depression jobless, and provide purchasing power to drain the surplus of food and manufactured goods piled up in warehouses throughout the country.

"What hit me?" wonders the New Deal (right), caught by a whirlwind decision of the Supreme Court.

VICTORIOUS BROTHERS, *Aaron (left) and Alex Schechter, shoulder lawyer Joseph Heller who won their celebrated lawsuit—the "Sick Chicken Case," a deathblow to the NRA. The government had indicted the brothers, poultry dealers in Brooklyn, New York, for breaking the NRA's "Live Poultry Code" that fostered fair competition. In turn the brothers had claimed that the NRA was unlawful, because Congress had improperly delegated too much legislative power to the President. In 1935 on a day New Dealers called "Black Monday," the Court killed the NRA (***Schechter Poultry Corp. v. U. S.***) and ruled against the Administration in two other important cases. In decisions that followed, the Court continued to strike down Roosevelt's major New Deal legislation.*

LINGERING REMNANT OF NRA: *A "Blue Eagle" poster (below) peels away at the hand of an employee in the Commerce Department, Washington, D. C. Until the Court outlawed the NRA, industries that had voluntarily tried to improve the economy by regulation of production and prices had displayed the "Eagle."*

we operate under approved code and display the Blue Eagle as a symbol of cooperation

Again the Supreme Court reviewed a conviction; again Justice Jackson wrote the majority opinion. The trial judge had properly instructed the jury, he said, to decide if Hans Haupt meant only to help his son or if he meant to help Germany against the United States. The jury had found him a traitor, and in law they had sufficient evidence.

"JURORS—PLAIN PEOPLE—have manfully stood up in the defense of liberty" on many occasions, wrote Justice Black in 1955. To deprive 3,000,000 persons of the safeguards in trial by jury went beyond the power of Congress, he declared; a law to do so was unconstitutional, and Miss Audrey M. Toth had won against Donald A. Quarles, Secretary of the Air Force.

Honorably discharged from military service in December, 1952, her brother Robert came home to Pittsburgh and got a job in a steel plant. Air Force police arrested him at work in May, 1953, and flew him to Korea for court-martial on charges of murdering a Korean the previous September.

At Miss Toth's petition, a district court issued a writ of habeas corpus, and the Air Force brought back its prisoner. A court of appeals ruled against him, and then the Supreme Court took the case.

Like Toth, any veteran might be hustled off for court-martial "for any alleged of-

fense" in service, Black warned—if the Court found power for Congress to say so. The Court did not. To provide for justice in such cases, said Black, Congress could give jurisdiction to civilian courts by law.

At an Air Force base in Oxfordshire, England, a sergeant's wife was saying she had killed her husband the night before.

Delusions, thought the Air Force psychiatrist; he knew how she had grown up wretched in a poor and broken home, how her husband squandered money and drank. But he sent men to investigate; they found her husband's body.

Under psychiatric and prenatal care, she waited in a hospital until a court-martial convicted her of premeditated murder and sentenced her to life at hard labor. Flown back to America in 1953, she bore her third child in a federal prison for women.

The Court of Military Appeals ordered a new trial; in 1955 doctors found her sane; then the Supreme Court agreed to hear argument that the Uniform Code of Military Justice denied her constitutional rights to a jury trial under the Sixth Amendment. With her case they took another that raised the same legal issues.

Working under pressure as the term was closing, the Court reached these cases and announced the validity of military trials for civilian dependents abroad. Warren, Black,

CARTOONS PRO AND CON *appeared in news-papers when President Franklin D. Roosevelt tried to add six Justices who would favor his policies. From 1935 until 1937, the Supreme Court pictured below negated New Deal attempts to lift a depressed economy.*

COURTESY JERRY DOYLE

"NINE OLD MEN" OF 1937: *From left are (standing) Owen J. Roberts, Pierce Butler, Harlan Fiske Stone, Benjamin N. Cardozo; (seated) Louis D. Brandeis, Willis J. Van Devanter, Chief Justice Charles Evans Hughes, James C. McReynolds, George Sutherland.*

STEEL LABOR

THE VOICE OF THE STEEL WORKERS ORGANIZING COMMITTEE — C.I.O.

MAY 15, 1937   Price Two Cents   43   VOL. II, No. 9

25,000 J & L MEN STRIKE FOR SIGNED CONTRACT

STEEL MILLS TELL SWOC TO CALL STRIKE

Youngstown Sheet & Tube and Republic Workers Demand Contracts

Youngstown, Ohio, May 15.—Delegates of steel union lodges in the Youngstown area have empowered the Steel Workers Organizing Committee, headed by Philip M ... call strikes in ...Sheet ...

AN ACT OF BAD FAITH
★ ★ ★ ★   ★ ★ ★ ★

A Statement to the Public on the Steel Crisis, by Philip Murray, Chairman of the Steel Workers Organizing Committee

THERE is a crisis developing on certain "fronts" of the steel industry, as regards management's relations with its workmen, which is of vital interest to the general public. I want the public to know that responsibility for any strike that might take place rests solely with those so-called "big independents" who refuse to give their own workmen the protection they want through a written contract.

To those who might not have been following closely the present successful campaign of the Steel Workers Organizing Committee, I wish ... ...nificant fact... ...de o ...

MURRAY CALLS 'WAR' BOARD OF OTHER PLANTS

Jones & Laughlin Refusal to Sign Contract Is Cause of Walkout

Pittsburgh, Pa., May 15.—When Jones & Laughlin Steel Corporation officials refused to sign a SWOC contract 25,000 workmen in Pittsburgh and Aliquippa works of the corporation ... went on strike. Picket lin... ...n around the mill ...ight and after

AFTERMATH OF A COURT DECISION: *A steel strike in Pittsburgh (right) in May, 1937, followed a Supreme Court case involving Jones & Laughlin Steel Corporation. Its plant in Aliquippa had fired 12 employees who supported the Steel Workers Organizing Committee, a C.I.O. union. When the Court upheld the Wagner Act, which forbids such action by management, it ordered the workers reinstated. The Court's action confirmed labor's right to vote for the union of its choice. But at first the company refused to consent to an election. Workers went on strike and won. Steelworker (below) casts ballot for union preference.*

and Douglas noted dissent; Frankfurter, a "reservation" of opinion.

Then, as it rarely does, the Court granted a petition for rehearing; in 1957 six Justices agreed to reverse the decisions. Congress could not deprive civilians of the safeguards in the Bill of Rights, Black insisted. Under the new ruling, courts-martial may not try mothers, wives, or children of servicemen for crimes carrying a death penalty.

Extending this rule in a series of cases, the Court stopped court-martial trial of dependents for lesser crimes, and of civilian employees abroad for all crimes.

MEANWHILE, in another long series of decisions, the Court was defining the constitutional rules for fair criminal trials in state courts.

Tortured and whipped by deputy sheriffs, three men confessed to murder; in 1936 the Supreme Court found that their state, Mississippi, had denied them due process of law.

Held for days against Indiana law, questioned for hours by relays of policemen, a man named Watts finally said something that convicted him of murder; in 1949 the Court ruled that such coercion also denies due process—if a man's own words may cost his life he must speak at his own choice.

For himself and a codefendant, a man named Griffin wrote a petition: because of their "porverty," they could not pay for a transcript of their trial for armed robbery and without this record they could not appeal in Illinois courts. Griffin thought the Fourteenth Amendment forbade justice "only for 'Rich.'" So did the Justices, in 1956. They ordered Illinois to give Griffin a free transcript; they gave "equal protection of the laws" a new value. If a man with money can buy a hearing because his state offers a right of appeal, that state must help a man without money.

Accused of breaking into a poolroom in Panama City, Florida, in 1961, Clarence Earl Gideon tried to get a court-appointed lawyer, and failed. He tried to defend himself, and failed. He tried to persuade the Supreme Court to review his case, and succeeded. The Court appointed Abe Fortas of Washington to argue Gideon's claim that without a lawyer no man gets the fair trial the Constitution demands.

Before the Justices, Fortas stressed the confusion any layman would feel when Florida said: "Apply the doctrine of *Mapp* v. *Ohio*. Construe this statute of the State of Florida. Cross-examine witnesses. Call your own witnesses. Argue to the jury."

Florida's attorney argued that the issue should be left to the states. But all nine Justices agreed that no man should have to defend himself against a felony charge, trying to apply precedents he never heard of and construe laws he never read. If a defendant has no money for a lawyer, the state court must appoint one for him. On retrial, a Florida jury acquitted Gideon.

As Justice Potter Stewart had pointed out, Florida wouldn't have let Gideon represent anyone else as an advocate in its courts. But as lawyers and newspapers said, in the Supreme Court Gideon could stand for anyone who happened to be poor.

DOLLREE MAPP may stand for anyone who thinks a government should obey its own laws.

To protect the people's right to security, the Fourth Amendment requires federal officers to have specific and detailed warrants for searches and arrests. The states have had similar requirements.

But for many years officers disregarded this. If they broke into a home and seized property contrary to law, prosecutors could use it as evidence in court to convict its owner—government could, and did, break the law to its own advantage.

In 1914 the Supreme Court announced that if federal officers seize things illegally, federal judges must not admit such things in evidence in their courtrooms. But that decision did not bind state courts. Until 1961 the Court left states free to admit such evidence if they chose.

When police arrived at Mrs. Mapp's home in Cleveland, Ohio, on May 23, 1957, she refused to admit them unless they had a warrant. Three hours later they forced a door, handcuffed Mrs. Mapp for being "belligerent," and searched the house thoroughly, hunting for a person "wanted for questioning" and for evidence of gambling. Finding books they thought obscene, they arrested her for having these.

LIKE FATHER LIKE SON AND DAUGHTER, *William and Lillian Gobitas with their father, Walter, between them, believe as Jehovah's Witnesses that saluting the flag is idolatry. Their father charged that compulsory pledges of allegiance to the flag denied his children freedom of religion, a basic constitutional right. In 1940 the Court ruled against him, refusing to be "school board for the country."*

HANDS AT HER SIDES, *nine-year-old Jana Gobitas (center) abstains from saluting the flag in the third-grade classroom of Bayside School, Milwaukee, Wisconsin, in 1965.*

Unlike her father, William, a fifth grader in the picture taken in 1935 (above, right), Jana never faced expulsion from school for refusing the salute.

In 1943 the Court reversed its ruling in the Gobitas case and said: "Compelling the flag salute and pledge . . . invades the sphere of intellect and spirit which it is the purpose of the First Amendment . . . to reserve from all official control."

On trial, Mrs. Mapp offered evidence that a boarder had left the books, some clothes, and no forwarding address. The police did not prove they had ever had any warrant. But Mrs. Mapp got a prison sentence. Ohio's highest court upheld it.

Reviewing *Mapp* v. *Ohio,* the Supreme Court decided in 1961 to bar the doors of every courtroom—state as well as federal—"to evidence secured by official lawlessness." The Fourth Amendment sets standards for search and seizure, said its opinion, and the Fourteenth requires judges to uphold them in every state of the Union. In closing the courtroom doors, the Justices guarded the doors of every home.

AS THE UNITED STATES ENTERED the second half of the 20th century, forces were gathering which would lead in a few short years to a historic reversal. Since 1896 the "separate but equal" doctrine upheld by the Supreme Court in *Plessy* v. *Ferguson* had been the law of the land; under it many states and the District of Columbia had operated racially segregated school systems.

The beginnings of change were deceptively modest. In 1951 Oliver Brown of Topeka, Kansas, sued the city school board in behalf of his eight-year-old daughter Linda Carol. She had to cross railroad yards to catch the bus for a black school 21 blocks away; her father wanted her in the white school only five blocks from home.

Three federal judges heard testimony on teachers,

ROUNDUP OF ALIENS *in World War II (below) begins an evacuation of persons of Japanese ancestry from west coast military zones. The government shipped the civilians to detention centers like Owens Valley in California (right). More than 110,000 Japanese-Americans endured bleak camp life; one of them painted the picture above.*

FIGHTER *for civil liberty, Dr. Gordon K. Hirabayashi (right), teaches a class at the University of Alberta in Canada. A college senior in 1942, he refused to obey a military order that required Japanese-Americans to register for evacuation to relocation centers. He claimed that the Army order violated his rights as a U. S. citizen. His plea failed when the Supreme Court (**Hirabayashi v. U. S.**) held that the threat of invasion and sabotage sanctioned the military restriction of constitutional rights among Japanese-American citizens.*

courses of study, buildings; they heard lawyers for Brown and 12 other black parents argue that the Kansas law permitting segregation violated the Fourteenth Amendment. Finding the schools substantially equal, the judges ruled against Brown; they said that *Plessy* controlled the case.

Ten-year-old Harry Briggs, Jr., and 66 other black children had filed a similar suit, through their parents, against school authorities in Clarendon County, South Carolina. The county was spending $395,000 for 2,375 white pupils, $282,000 for 6,531 black pupils. All the white students had desks; two black schools had no desks at all.

The federal court that heard the *Briggs* case ordered Clarendon County to "equalize" its schools as soon as possible; but, relying on *Plessy,* it refused to order black pupils admitted to white schools, or to rule South Carolina's segregation law invalid.

The Supreme Court heard argument in December, 1952, on the *Brown* and the *Briggs* cases, combining them with an almost identical case from Prince Edward County, Virginia, and one from Delaware.

Delaware's court of equity had found separate black schools inferior and ordered black children transferred to white schools at once; its highest court had sustained the order, and school officials had sought review in the Supreme Court.

Briefs for all the black litigants included data from psychologists and social scientists. Since Brandeis filed his famous brief for Oregon in 1908, lawyers had offered "nonlegal" facts to defend a challenged law; now they offered such material to attack state laws. Records from the lower courts printed the testimony of expert witnesses explaining why they thought legal segregation harmed black children.

In June, 1953, the Court ordered a reargument. Then, on September 8, Chief Justice Fred M. Vinson, aged 63, died unexpectedly of a heart attack. President Eisenhower moved promptly to appoint his successor, Earl Warren, the popular Governor of California. The reargument proceeded on schedule in December with 51 *amicus curiae,* "friend of the court," briefs—a record number up to that time.

On May 17, 1954, Chief Justice Warren read the momentous opinion for a unanimous Court: ". . . in the field of public education the doctrine of 'separate but equal' has no place." The Court ruled that segregation in public schools deprives children of "the equal protection of the laws guaranteed by the Fourteenth Amendment."

The May 1954 rulings affected 21 states and the District of Columbia. But the Justices did not order specific changes at once. They gave all the states affected a chance to be heard in yet another argument, this one on appropriate remedies.

Some states filed briefs. Oklahoma explained that it would have to rewrite its tax laws; North Carolina and Florida included long reports on public opinion.

On May 31, 1955, the Chief Justice again spoke for a unanimous Court. The cases would go back to the lower courts; these would review the work of local officials facing the problem of unprecedented change. Desegregation would now proceed "with all deliberate speed."

TAXATION without representation is tyranny, American colonists were saying angrily in the 1760's. In the 1960's, voters in American cities were saying the same thing.

City voters sent some lawmakers to Congress and the state legislatures, of course; but in many states rural voters—a minority of the population—sent more. People had been moving from farms to cities, but electoral districts had not changed.

In 1950, one Vermont representative spoke for 49 people, another for 33,155. In Connecticut, a mere 9½ percent of the people could elect a majority of the state's representatives. By 1955, the Colorado legislature was giving Denver $2.3 million a year in school aid for 90,000 children; it was giving a semirural county $2.4 million for 18,000 pupils.

Although the Supreme Court had decided cases on voting frauds and discrimination in state primary elections, it had dismissed a case on Congressional apportionment in 1946. "Courts ought not to enter this political thicket," Justice Frankfurter had warned; federal judges had obeyed.

Nevertheless, Charles W. Baker of Memphis, Tennessee, and nine other qualified

FORMER AIR FORCE POLICEMAN *Robert Toth hugs his mother and sister on his return to the United States from Korea. He had been honorably discharged from the service in 1952 only to be arrested by the Air Force the following year. Charged in the death of a Korean civilian shot by an Air Force sentry one night when Toth was on guard duty, the former airman was flown back to Korea to face a military trial. Toth went free when the Supreme Court held that ex-servicemen may not be tried by court-martial for alleged service crimes (**Toth v. Quarles**).*

voters filed a suit against Joe C. Carr, Secretary of State, and other officials. They asked a federal court to order changes in the state's election procedure. The Tennessee constitution said electoral districts should be changed every ten years, but the General Assembly had not passed a reapportionment law since 1901.

When the lower court dismissed *Baker* v. *Carr,* the Supreme Court accepted it. The Justices studied briefs with maps of voting districts, and a special brief for the United States; they heard argument twice. Then, setting precedents aside, the Court decided that minority rule in state legislatures is a matter for judges to review.

Justice Brennan spoke for the majority. If a state lets one person's vote count for more than another's because they live in different districts, that state denies its citizens equal protection of the laws. Citizens wronged by "debasement of their votes" may go to court for help.

In March, 1962, the Supreme Court sent Baker's case back to the district judges for them to decide. By November, voters in 30 of the 50 states were suing in state as well as federal courts for new voting districts.

A case from Georgia brought the issue of Congressional apportionment before the Supreme Court again; it ruled in 1964 that Congressional districts should be equal in population.

Alabama appealed to the Supreme Court

LESSONS IN EQUALITY: *When a white public school turned away Linda Brown (left, later Mrs. Charles D. Smith, of Topeka, Kansas), her father contended that segregated public schools could not provide equal opportunities. Such discrimination infringed his daughter's constitutional rights, he claimed. The resulting case became the most famous in modern Court history. In 1954, unanimously overruling the "separate but equal" decision of the 1896* **Plessy v. Ferguson** *case, the Court shed new light on the "equal protection of the laws" provision of the Fourteenth Amendment. In public systems, the Court concluded: "Separate educational facilities are inherently unequal"* (**Brown v. Board of Education**). *This ruling affected 21 states with segregated schoolrooms such as the one at right. It also spurred a revolution in the legal status of blacks in all avenues of life. In 1975, because of this decision, sixth-grader Charles and fifth-grader Kimberly attend desegregated neighborhood schools—with classrooms like the one below.*

when district judges rejected three reapportionment plans for the state. Sustaining the lower court, the Justices listed new rules for a state legislature. Both houses must be based on population, they said; and if districts differ in population, the Court would not find the differences valid for geographic, historic, or economic reasons alone.

"ALMIGHTY GOD, we acknowledge our dependence upon Thee, and we beg Thy blessings upon us, our parents, our teachers and our Country."

As supervisors of the state's public education under New York law, the Board of Regents wrote this classroom prayer in 1951. Formal religion has no place in public schools, they said, but "teaching our children, as set forth in the Declaration of Independence, that Almighty God is their Creator" would give the "best security" in dangerous days. They recommended their prayer to local school boards; some accepted it, including the board in New Hyde Park, which voted in 1958 for the prayer to open each school day.

Some parents objected; they feared that if government may regulate or require any religious practice in a public school it gains power over matters that should be free. Steven I. Engel and four other parents asked a New York court to order the prayer discontinued.

William J. Vitale, Jr., and other board members replied that prayer gave moral training for good citizenship. On request, they said, any child would be excused from praying.

By adopting the Regents' prayer, schools did not prefer or teach religion, the courts in New York held; but schools must not compel any child to pray. In 1961 the Supreme

103

NATIONAL ARCHIVES (OPPOSITE) AND HUGO HARPER

Court accepted *Engel* v. *Vitale* for review.

Justice Black gave the Supreme Court's opinion in June, 1962: A "solemn avowal of divine faith," the Regents' prayer was indeed religious—and unconstitutional, because the authors of the Constitution thought religion "too personal, too sacred, too holy," for any civil magistrate to sanction. No government should compose official prayers for Americans to recite.

When lawyers for two other school boards appeared before the Court in 1963, they praised the ruling in *Engel* v. *Vitale* but insisted that it did not apply to their cases. In their schools official prayers had no place, although pupils read the Holy Bible and recited the Lord's Prayer every day unless parents wanted them excused.

Professed atheists, Mrs. Madalyn E. Murray of Baltimore and her son William challenged the school exercises for favoring belief over nonbelief. Mr. and Mrs. Edward L. Schempp of Abington, Pennsylvania, wanted to teach their children Unitarian beliefs without "contradictory" practices at school. As taxpayers and parents of students, they had standing to sue.

Reviewing these two cases, the Supreme Court declared again that no state may prescribe religious ceremonies in its schools, that the Constitution stands between the government and the altar.

PUBLIC ANGER over the Supreme Court's powers and decisions ran high in Marshall's day and in Taney's, and again during the New Deal period of the 1930's, when Charles Evans Hughes was Chief Justice. Not so long ago, billboards and bumper stickers called for Congress to impeach Earl Warren; attacks on the Court still smolder and occasionally flare.

Such turmoil comes when the Nation confronts new difficulties and new dangers, as well as new notions of what freedom means. The Justices review a critical case arising under the Constitution, as citizens debate the issues it involves.

Critics have accused the Court of pampering Communists and criminals. Southerners have denounced its rulings on race and civil rights; fresh protest has come from northern metropolises, both from the white suburbs and the inner-city ghettos. Legislators have debated constitutional amendments to overrule the Court on reapportionment. Some clergymen and laymen have charged that the Court favors godlessness, corruption of young minds by smut, murder of the innocent unborn.

With equal force and passion, others have answered that the Court should decide such cases as these, and have insisted that it has decided them rightly.

Through all its history, the Supreme Court has been the ultimate guardian of the rights we enjoy and the obligations we accept as a free people. As the Constitution moves into its third century, it must continue to be reaffirmed and reapplied to the most fundamental issues arising in an ever-changing society in an equally changing world.

In 1969, Chief Justice Warren stepped down after presiding over the Court for 16 years, a period marked by controversial decisions and impassioned public debate. There were heated conflicts over desegregation remedies formulated under the decision in *Brown* v. *Board of Education;* over what was called a revolution in the rights of criminals; and over issues of religious freedom, guaranteed in the first 16 words of the Bill of Rights.

Warren's successor, Warren Burger, a native of Minnesota, had been a judge of the Court of Appeals for the District of Columbia Circuit for more than a decade. When Burger stepped down in 1986, he had served longer than any Chief Justice appointed in the 20th century. President Reagan, as several of his predecessors had done, turned to the Court itself for the new Chief Justice: He named William H. Rehnquist, an Associate Justice since 1972.

WOMEN'S RIGHTS have become such a dominant thread in the fabric of our political, social, and judicial life that it is hard to realize how recently this pattern was established. Not until 1971 did the Supreme Court first hold a government classification by gender unconstitutional; in the following years cases involving charges of sex discrimination have become a more commonplace item on the Court's docket.

Decision by decision, the Supreme Court struck down laws that arbitrarily favored males over females. Starting with *Reed* v. *Reed* in 1971, the Court said that the choice of administrator for an estate "may not lawfully be mandated solely on the basis of sex." In 1973, the Court invalidated a federal law that provided broader housing and medical benefits for males in the military than it did for females. In 1974 an equal-pay-for-equal-work statute was upheld.

In 1975, the Court was faced with another aspect of discrimination and decreed that

PLEA OF A PAUPER: *Clarence Earl Gideon (opposite) signs copies of* Gideon's Trumpet, *the story of a case that heralded new hope for destitute defendants. Charged with breaking into a poolroom, penniless when brought to trial, Gideon asked the court to appoint counsel. But the judge refused, saying that Florida law provided indigent defendants with counsel only if they faced the possibility of the death sentence. Convicted, Gideon spent hours in the prison library consulting law books. Then he penciled the petition (right) asking the Supreme Court to hear his case. The Court appointed attorney Abe Fortas to represent him. In 1963, it decided Gideon had been denied a fair trial, adding that every state must provide counsel to an indigent charged with a felony (Gideon v. Wainwright). Later, in a retrial, his lawyer won acquittal for Gideon.*

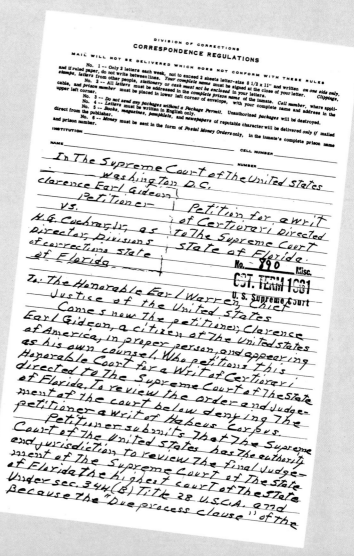

widowers with small children are entitled to Social Security survivors' benefits equal to those of widows in similar situations. Finally, in 1976, the Court held that discrimination against men was just as much a violation of the Constitution as discrimination against women. This decision involved an Oklahoma statute permitting women to buy beer at the age of 18 but denying men the same right until they reached the age of 21.

Not all decisions of the Court have satisfied feminists. In 1979 it upheld a Massachusetts law giving preference to veterans in state employment. Even though more men than women could take advantage of the provision, there was no intent to discriminate by sex, said the Court; women veterans were fully included. Justice Marshall, joined by Justice Brennan, dissented, saying "this degree of preference is not constitutionally permissible." Then, on June 25, 1981, the Court upheld an all-male military draft registration law. The president of the National Organization for Women said the decision perpetuated "the myth of this country that all men are better than all women."

Rapid social change has greatly affected the law in the area of sex discrimination. In 1982, the Court held that a state university

nursing school, which had historically admitted only women, could not exclude a male applicant simply on the basis of sex. In 1984, a unanimous Court held that a federal law banning discrimination based on sex and race was applicable to law-firm hiring and promotion decisions.

Two years later, in an opinion written by Justice Rehnquist, the Court held unanimously that sexual harassment in the workplace is forbidden. Then, in 1987, and again by a unanimous decision, the Court upheld a California antibias law under which a local club of Rotary International moved to admit women—despite the organization's long-standing policy of admitting men only.

JUDGE FRED WOODS

FREEDOM OF RELIGION, guaranteed by the First Amendment, has been reaffirmed frequently by the Supreme Court. Yet virtually every term brings new and often highly charged religious issues.

One of the most famous of the Court's rulings involving the conflict between religious freedom and state public schools came in 1972. It resulted in a victory for three Amish families in rural Wisconsin who were testing the guarantee of religious freedom. They had refused to send their children to public school beyond the eighth grade, asserting that modern secondary education was contrary to the Amish religion and a threat to their children's salvation. "The Amish . . . have convincingly demonstrated the sincerity of their religious beliefs," said the Court, and the children were free, after completing elementary school, to follow the centuries-old tradition of learning at home.

When the Internal Revenue Service declared in 1970 that private schools discriminating against blacks could no longer claim tax-exempt status, the action went largely unnoticed by the public. In 1983, it became prime-time news when two religious schools having admission policies based on race sought to regain tax-favored status and the case reached the Supreme Court.

Counsel for Bob Jones University and Goldsboro Christian School argued that their policies were based on sincerely held religious beliefs. But the Court ruled that the First Amendment did not prevent denial of tax-favored status. Eliminating racial discrimination in education substantially outweighed any burden placed on the free exercise of religion, according to the eight-to-one majority.

The Court also held in 1983 that reading a prayer at the opening day session of the Nebraska legislature did not violate the First Amendment's establishment-of-religion clause. In another highly publicized case, a year later, it ruled that a Nativity scene displayed at Christmastime by the city of Pawtucket, Rhode Island, did not violate the Constitution. This extended the degree to which government may use religious symbols to acknowledge the Nation's heritage.

The long-standing controversy over religion in public schools took yet another form in 1985. The Court struck down an Alabama law that permitted a moment of silence in schools for prayer or meditation. Justice Stevens, speaking for the Court, said that the law had no secular purpose, but rather was designed to encourage students to pray.

In 1987, the Court faced the question of whether the state of Louisiana could require the teaching of "creation science" to accompany the teaching of evolution. By a seven-to-two majority, the Court held that Louisiana could not show a secular purpose for the creation-science law and thus the law failed the first test traditionally applied to determine whether an establishment-clause violation has occurred.

Through a series of decisions in recent years, the Court has ringingly reaffirmed freedom of conscience and religious practice. However, thorny questions remain, and new ones will arise. As in the past, the Court will continue to be called upon to decide issues that involve both strongly held religious beliefs and the hard realities of modern economic and political life.

MOST AMERICANS take freedom of speech and of the press as the most evident and absolute of rights, guaranteed by the First Amendment. Yet in the last two decades, the Supreme Court has been called upon to decide more cases concerning freedom of the press than in the previous 175 years. Controversies involving the press and the broadcast media are extensively reported by them, fairly in their own eyes and in

RELEASED FROM JAIL, *Jon Argersinger (opposite upper, at right) greets Attorney J. Michael Shea. Charged with carrying a concealed weapon and unable to afford a lawyer, Argersinger had no legal representation at his trial. At that time, Florida law provided counsel only to indigent defendants accused of felonies, in accordance with the* Gideon *decision. Argersinger asked Shea to appeal his conviction. Broadening and extending* Gideon, *the Supreme Court ruled in 1972 that "no person may be imprisoned for any offense" unless represented by counsel. As a court-appointed lawyer, Shea presents another client's case to a Florida judge in 1982 (opposite lower).*

those of some observers, not always so fairly in the eyes of others.

In the 1970's, the press was "subjected to a judicial battering that has been more serious and more fundamental, than the assaults that were mounted in more parlous days," an attorney representing press interests asserted in a 1979 weekly magazine article.

Free to reply to such criticism when he retired from the Court in 1981, Associate Justice Potter Stewart said that the notion that "traditional protections are being ignored or disregarded or destroyed is a completely fallacious thought."

Controversy over the Vietnam war was at a peak when, on June 13, 1971, the *New York Times* began publishing installments of a secret, illegally obtained document concerning the United States' conduct of the war. The government saw grave dangers to U.S. security in the publication of what became known as the Pentagon Papers, and sought injunctions to prevent both the *Times* and the *Washington Post* from further dissemination of the stolen information. Within two weeks the case reached the Supreme Court, which heard arguments on June 26 and announced its decision on June 30.

Once again, as it has through the years, the Court refused to countenance restraint prior to publication. In a brief decision, the Court observed that any system of prior restraint bears "a heavy presumption against its constitutional validity." Each Justice filed a separate opinion; there were three dissents. Among the majority, Justice Brennan denounced prior restraint in nearly absolute terms, but he conceded that in wartime there might be a "single, extremely narrow" class of exceptions. The three dissenters emphasized the "almost irresponsibly feverish" speed with which the case was disposed of; according to Justice Harlan, it should have been conducted under full ground rules.

The Pentagon Papers were published and were a journalistic sensation at home and abroad; but the war in Vietnam went on.

Do news reporters have a right to confidentiality of their sources under the First Amendment? They argue that unless they can protect the identity of people who give them information under promises of secrecy, the sources will dry up.

Not so, said the Court in 1972, speaking through Justice White; when a grand jury is seeking evidence concerning a crime, a reporter's sources are not necessarily protected. If the reporter believes the testimony is not essential to the case, he or she may ask the court to issue a protective order; but the Court will decide.

Another controversial issue involving First Amendment protection has reached the Supreme Court: the explicit treatment of sex in books, magazines, and motion pictures. In 1957, and again in 1966, the Court held that the First Amendment protects material challenged as pornography—even if the material might appeal to prurient interests and affront community standards—unless it is shown to be "utterly without redeeming social value." This test proved difficult to apply in practice, and in 1973 the Court substituted a modified standard: There is First Amendment protection unless "the work, taken as a whole, lacks serious literary, artistic, political, or scientific value." At the same time, the Court held that pornography cases should be decided by trial courts on the basis of individual community standards, not national ones.

But in 1982 the Court unanimously upheld a New York criminal statute prohibiting the distribution of material depicting sexual activity by children under the age of 16.

"ON THE EVENING of October 18, 1975, local police found the six members of the Henry Kellie family murdered in their home in Sutherland, Neb., a town of about

FOLLOWING A CENTURIES-OLD CUSTOM *of learning at home, an Amish boy strings a barbed-wire fence under his father's supervision. When three Amish families in Green County, Wisconsin, refused on religious grounds to send their children to school past the eighth grade, the fathers were convicted of violating the state's compulsory school education law and fined five dollars each. The Supreme Court invalidated the conviction in 1972. In this case, said the Court, the right to the free exercise of religion, guaranteed by the First Amendment, outweighed the interests of the state.*

1901

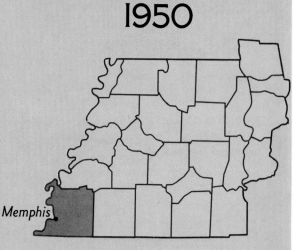

| 43,000 VOTERS | 43,000 VOTERS |
| 7 1/2 REPRESENTATIVES | 11 REPRESENTATIVES |

BATTLE OF THE BALLOT: *In 1901 Memphis, Tennessee, had as many people as eight nearby counties together and elected nearly the same number of representatives. By 1950 Memphis' population equaled that of 24 counties. Under the state constitution the city should have gained more representatives, but did not; so the rural vote counted almost four times as much as the urban. Reviewing city voters' complaint that this denied them equal protection of the laws, the Court in 1962 held that judges should hear and decide such claims under the Fourteenth Amendment (**Baker v. Carr**). Chief Justice Earl Warren looked back upon this as the most important and influential single decision in his 16 years on the Court. It opened the way to enunciation (in **Reynolds v. Sims**) of the "one person, one vote" principle and its enforcement by court order in many related cases across the Nation.*

1950

| 312,000 VOTERS | 312,000 VOTERS |
| 7 1/2 REPRESENTATIVES | 26 REPRESENTATIVES |

850 people." This stark recital began the decision that resolved two potentially conflicting guarantees in the Bill of Rights in favor of the First Amendment.

The day after the grisly discovery, Erwin Charles Simants was arrested and soon charged with committing the murders in the course of a sexual assault. The media gave the crime sensational coverage.

The right to a fair trial in all criminal prosecutions is explicitly guaranteed by the Sixth Amendment. The Nebraska Supreme Court sustained a lower court order restricting media coverage on the grounds that prejudicial news stories would make a fair trial for Simants difficult, if not impossible, anywhere in the state.

Unanimously, the Nation's highest court decided otherwise, again refusing to sanction prior restraint. The majority opinion affirmed the "explicit command" of the Constitution that "freedom to speak and publish shall not be abridged," echoing the trenchant phrases of Chief Justice Charles Evans Hughes half a century earlier in *Near* v. *Minnesota*.

Again and again in recent years, the Court has struck down state laws and lower court decisions that attempted to limit publication. In 1974 it ruled unanimously that the state of Florida could not require a newspaper to grant a "right of reply" to a candidate for public office whom the paper had criticized in print. In effect, such a law would give the state some control over the newspaper's content, a form of government compulsion the Court held unconstitutional.

In 1978 the Court determined that the Commonwealth of Virginia could not prohibit the accurate reporting of closed-door proceedings of a state commission inquiring into the conduct of a judge, a matter of "utmost public concern." In 1979, however, it held that the press did not have an absolute right to be present at pretrial proceedings. It sustained the lower court's exclusion of a reporter, saying that publication of the accused's confession would prevent a fair trial. The decision brought a barrage of criticism.

Criminal trials themselves are another matter, the Court said in regard to a Virginia murder case a year later, when it held that the right of the public and the press to attend

EIGHT-MAN COURT *of the October 1969 term illustrates the overlapping service of individual members. From left, seated: Justices Harlan (who served with two Chief Justices) and Black (who served with five); Chief Justice Burger; Justices Douglas (who served with five) and Brennan (with two). Standing: Justices Marshall, Stewart, and White (all with two). The seat vacated when Justice Fortas resigned remained empty while the Senate rejected two nominations by President Nixon; it was later filled by Justice Blackmun.*

them is guaranteed by the First and Fourteenth Amendments. The right to be present was specifically extended, in a unanimous decision in 1984, to the jury selection process for criminal trials.

In other First Amendment rulings of recent years the Court struck down laws placing restrictions on advertising by lawyers, taxing large newspapers on their use of ink and paper, and, perhaps appropriately, a federal law forbidding the use of picket signs and distribution of leaflets on the sidewalks adjoining the Supreme Court itself.

A CONSTITUTIONAL CRISIS seemed imminent on May 31, 1974, as the Watergate episode neared its climax. On that date, the Court granted a petition to hear a case whose outcome could lead to the impeachment of the President, and set July 8 for argument. The very name of the case spoke history and high drama: *United States,*

Petitioner v. *Richard M. Nixon, President of the United States.*

The House of Representatives was already considering impeachment proceedings against President Nixon based on his part in a cover-up. Seven former members of his staff had been indicted on felony charges. They were accused of conspiring to obstruct justice by concealing White House involvement in the 1972 break-in at Democratic Party offices in Washington's Watergate complex. The U. S. District Court ordered President Nixon to produce as evidence tape recordings and notes on 64 conversations that took place in the White House. The President refused to comply.

By 10 a.m. on July 8 it was evident that the 192 seats in the Court Chamber could not begin to accommodate the throngs who sought to witness this unique and critical passage in the life of the Republic. But more than 1,500 people attended at least part of the three hours of probing, measured, often quietly eloquent debate.

They heard the President's advocate, James D. St. Clair, pressed by insistent questions from the Justices, defend the claim of absolute Presidential privilege and immunity from court orders. Even in a criminal conspiracy? Yes, said the President's lawyer, "even if it's criminal."

They heard the Texas accents of Special Prosecutor Leon Jaworski as he invoked the constitutional power of the government to obtain evidence of a crime and also the structure of checks and balances. "Boiled down," he declared, "this case really presents one fundamental issue: Who is to be the arbiter of what the Constitution says?"

Two weeks later, on a gray and muggy July 24, a tense crowd again filled the Court Chamber. As the hands of the clock marked 11, the traditional cry of "Oyez!" rang out. With somber dignity the Chief Justice took note of the recent death of former Chief Justice Earl Warren, "our beloved colleague." Then he went on to read in measured tones his opinion for a unanimous Court. For 17 minutes the audience strained to capture every word of the unequivocal finding: The President must surrender the tapes.

"Narrow," some commentators called the decision. It was, in strongly reaffirming the separation of powers and the constitutional roots of executive privilege, but ruling that here the President's privilege must yield to the demands of a fair trial, equally guaranteed by the Constitution.

"Broad," others called it. It was, in reaffirming what Chief Justice John Marshall had said in *Marbury* v. *Madison* 171 years earlier—that it is "emphatically the province and duty" of this Court "to say what the law is." It also echoed a ruling by Marshall in 1807. Sitting on circuit in the trial of former Vice President Aaron Burr for treason, Marshall ordered President Jefferson to deliver to him secret military reports concerning Burr's alleged role in plotting war against the United States.

On August 9 President Nixon became the first chief executive in the Nation's history to

FEMALE ARMY PARATROOPER *trains alongside men, and a woman works on a telephone line. Women increasingly hold such nontraditional jobs. In 1971 the Supreme Court overturned a state law that gave preferential treatment to men over equally qualified women. (**Reed** v. **Reed**). In 1973 the Court assured females in the military the same benefits as males. Various employers have instituted affirmative action programs to reduce the effects of past discrimination. By refusing to review an appeals court decision, the Court in 1978 upheld programs at the American Telephone & Telegraph Company.*

resign. Publication of three conversations of the disputed 64 had brought his Presidency to an end. At noon that day, the Chief Justice administered the oath of office to Gerald R. Ford, the new President.

"THE MOST SIGNIFICANT constitutional ruling since *United States* v. *Nixon* nine years earlier," said a constitutional historian of an otherwise obscure immigration case decided in June, 1983. This time the powers of Congress were at issue, going to the heart of the Constitution's separation of powers among the executive, legislative, and judicial branches.

The case lacked the drama and popular interest of Watergate but was, said some observers, far broader in its effect. At stake was the constitutionality of the "legislative veto," a device used by Congress since 1932 in some 350 legislative acts. In nearly 200 laws still in effect, Congress had delegated powers to the executive branch while retaining the authority to veto the way in which the powers were exercised by departments, agencies, and commissions.

Jagdish Chadha, an Indian born in Kenya and holding a British passport, had been ordered to leave the United States after obtaining a university degree in Ohio. He appealed to the Immigration and Naturalization Service and eventually obtained permission to remain as a hardship case. But the House subcommittee reviewing a list of aliens seeking permanent residence disagreed and removed his name. Chadha fought back with the help of a law firm that appealed his case through the courts. Nine

RIGHT TO LIFE OR RIGHT TO CHOOSE? *Demonstrations across the country continue more than a decade after the Supreme Court ruled on abortion. Denied abortions by state statutes, a woman in Texas and another in Georgia endured frustrating legal battles before their cases reached the Supreme Court. In 1973 the Court struck down the statutes as unduly restricting the Fourteenth Amendment guarantees of personal liberty and the related right to privacy* (**Roe** v. **Wade** *and* **Doe** v. **Bolton**). *But the Court has since ruled that Congress can limit the use of federal funds for abortions.*

years later it reached the supreme tribunal.

The decision of Congress to deport Chadha was a legislative act, Chief Justice Burger held in his opinion for the Court, and the subcommittee's "one-house veto" was unlawful. It violated "the Framers' decision that the legislative power of the Federal Government be exercised in accord with a single, finely wrought and exhaustively considered, procedure."

All legislation must be passed by both the House and the Senate and be presented to the President before becoming law, the opinion said. These procedures were designed to provide "enduring checks" on each branch and to maintain the separation of powers; "the carefully defined limits on the power of each Branch must not be eroded," the Court said.

Justice White, who was joined by Justice Rehnquist in dissent, reading his opinion aloud from the bench to give it added emphasis, described the veto as "a central means by which Congress secures the accountability of executive and independent agencies." The legislative veto, he said, is a useful invention for "the modern administrative state," enabling Congress to delegate authority while retaining responsibility.

"Not since the New Deal collisions of the 1930s," said one national publication, "had Congress felt so keenly the power of the Court to curtail its actions," thus altering the "delicate balance" of power between the legislative and executive branches.

But the Court's last words on the matter were definitive: "With all the obvious flaws of delay, untidiness, and potential for abuse, we have not yet found a better way to preserve freedom than by making the exercise of power subject to the carefully crafted restraints spelled out in the Constitution."

LIFE ITSELF is weighed on the scales of justice when a crime is punishable by death. On one side of the scales are the rights of the accused, protected in the body of the Constitution and in no fewer than five Amendments. On the other side is society's need, loudly and frequently voiced in an era of mounting crime and violence, to deter and punish criminals.

On the constitutionality of capital punish-

ment, the Court has spoken firmly in landmark cases. In *Furman* v. *Georgia,* announced on June 29, 1972, it found that the death penalty as applied in that case would be "cruel and unusual punishment," forbidden by the Eighth Amendment. For 631 men and 2 women waiting on death row in 32 states, the decision brought hope for new sentences or new trials.

More than half the states moved to rewrite their statutes to conform with the decision. The rewritten laws also came up for scrutiny; and in 1976 the Court cleared the air and flatly rejected the claim that the death sentence is in itself always cruel and unusual punishment. The Court upheld three of the new laws and invalidated two others. It held that the Eighth Amendment requires the sentencing judge or jury to consider not only the crime but also the individual character of the offender, as well as any mitigating circumstances in the case.

The Court went a step further in 1977. In a case involving the rape of an adult woman, it found the death sentence "grossly disproportionate and excessive" and thus unconsti-

tutional. Two Justices dissented strongly, characterizing rape as among the crimes constitutionally within the power of legislatures to make punishable by execution.

Since then a divided Court has refused to overturn the death penalty as such in a number of cases, with Justices Brennan and Marshall consistently dissenting from any imposition of capital punishment. However, in 1986 the Court held that the Eighth Amendment prevents states from executing insane convicts.

Further, said the Court by a six-to-three majority in 1987, mandatory death-sentence laws are never constitutional. In the same term, however, it modified an earlier ruling and said that accomplices in a murder, as well as the actual "triggerman," may be sentenced to death; and it rejected, by a five-to-four vote, statistical evidence that Georgia's system of capital punishment was tainted by racial discrimination.

Partly because of cases pending in the Supreme Court, there were no executions in the United States from 1968 through 1976. In the 11 years following, under state laws revised to accord with Supreme Court rulings, more than 90 persons convicted of violent crimes were put to death.

THE RIGHT OF DEFENDANTS charged with felonies to be represented by counsel, regardless of whether they could afford it, was extended to all state courts in the highly publicized *Gideon* decision of 1963. Less widely known is the decision concerning Jon Richard Argersinger, who had been sentenced by a Florida court to 90 days in prison for carrying a concealed weapon. In responding to his appeal in 1972, the Court expanded the right to counsel well beyond *Gideon*. Under this holding, an accused person may not be sent to prison, even on a misdemeanor charge, unless represented by an attorney; and the state must provide one for indigent defendants.

The exclusionary rule highlights the controversy between advocates of the rights of persons accused of crime and champions of the right of a society to protect itself. This rule, established and refined by a series of Court interpretations over the years, is little understood by the public. Among judges, attorneys, scholars, and legislators, it is a keenly debated and divisive issue, and it is

significant, often decisive, in the outcome of serious criminal cases.

The rule prescribes that evidence obtained by illegal means—including confessions obtained in violation of the *Miranda* warning requirement, conversations overheard through unauthorized electronic "bugging," or tangible evidence such as drugs or weapons improperly seized—may not be used in trials.

But in recent years, while repeatedly upholding the Amendment against unreasonable search and seizure and the *Miranda* rule, the Court has modified their application in some respects. In 1984, in *New York v. Quarles,* it created a "public safety" exception to *Miranda* in circumstances where the public is in immediate danger, allowing police officers to ask questions to remove a threat without first informing an arrested person of his rights.

During the same term it adopted a "good faith" exception to the exclusionary rule. This allowed evidence to be used if police conducting the search reasonably relied upon a search warrant later determined to be technically defective.

In 1987, in an opinion by Chief Justice Rehnquist, the Court upheld provisions of a 1984 law which, under specified circumstances, allows criminals to be held in custody while awaiting trial, rather than to be freed on bail.

ABORTION is one of the most emotional and divisive issues in contemporary America. The controversy reached the Supreme Court as a constitutional question in 1972; and on January 22, 1973, in what has been called a sweeping decision, the Court set limits on state power to prohibit or to regulate abortion. In deciding *Roe* v. *Wade* and *Doe* v. *Bolton,* it held prohibitory statutes in Texas and Georgia invalid, and with them the abortion laws of many other states.

Based upon its determination of when a fetus becomes viable, the Court ruled that for the first three months of pregnancy a state must leave the decision on abortion to the woman and her physician. For the stage beginning with the fourth month, the state may set regulations reasonably related to maternal health. Finally, for the stage after viability—around the seventh month—the state may prohibit abortion unless the mother's health is endangered.

Two dissenters called this decision an "extravagant exercise of raw judicial power." In the majority opinion, citing rights protected by the Ninth and Fourteenth Amendments, Justice Blackmun acknowledged the Court's full awareness "of the deep and seemingly absolute convictions that the subject inspires."

As demonstrators made their views known with marches and banners near the Supreme Court and on the avenues of the city, the Court reaffirmed its landmark ruling 13 years later by a five-to-four majority. It struck down a Pennsylvania statute that admittedly was intended to discourage women from choosing abortions.

Other decisions have upheld some state laws imposing medical and procedural requirements prior to abortion, but have ruled unconstitutional "unreasonable" requirements, such as the consent of the father of an unborn child or of the parents of a pregnant minor. The Court has also ruled that while all abortions cannot be constitutionally prohibited, Congress can deny use of federal funds to finance them.

But the clash of "deep and seemingly absolute convictions" goes on in both the public and legal arenas.

AFFIRMATIVE ACTION programs designed to redress discrimination based on race, religion, sex, or national origin have been repeatedly upheld by the Supreme Court, with some qualifications, since school segregation was outlawed in 1954 and a new Civil Rights Law was adopted by Congress in 1964.

The thorny issues involved have reached the Court in a stream of varied cases. One of the first to draw great national attention was that of "reverse discrimination" charged by Allan Bakke, which reached the high tribunal in 1977. Bakke, white, contested the denial of his admission to the medical school of the University of California at Davis, which reserved 16 of 100 places annually for minority candidates. Under this quota system, said Bakke, he had not been admitted, despite the fact that minority candidates with lower scores were accepted. He argued that this was a clear case of discrimination.

Bakke's counsel told the Court that his client's exclusion violated both the equal-protection clause of the Fourteenth Amendment and the Civil Rights Act of 1964. The latter prohibits the exclusion of anyone on the basis of race or color from any program receiving financial assistance from the federal government.

The implications for minorities, for all student admissions policies, and for the future of civil rights legislation were portentous. News coverage and speculation reached an intensity unknown since the Nixon tapes case; some people saw the whole process of desegregation threatened if Bakke's position were upheld.

On June 28, 1978, the Court spoke—to a crowded room and to an international audience beyond. That the Justices held strong individual views was clear; there were six separate opinions. By a vote of five to four, the Court determined that Allan Bakke should be admitted to the medical school at Davis. The Court also repudiated the school's quota system as such, but permitted some consideration of minority status to achieve diversity in graduate and professional school education. Supporters of more categorical positions on both sides criticized the holdings; but, in the judgment of a distinguished legal scholar, they "accomplished the task of defusing tension in a country which had become taut with anticipation."

A year later, by a five-to-two vote, the Court upheld affirmative action programs established by private employers and unions to end discrimination. In 1980 the Court narrowly sustained an act of Congress which set aside 10 percent of local public works programs for a defined category of minority businesses. Toward the goal of equality of economic opportunity, the opinion said, Congress has the "necessary latitude to try new techniques such as the limited use of racial and ethnic criteria."

Indeed, the use of racial quotas to redress deliberate past discrimination is permissible under some circumstances, the Court said in 1986 and again in 1987. In the latter case, it upheld a lower court's order to Alabama authorities to promote one qualified black state trooper for every white trooper promoted until a nondiscriminatory promotion procedure was established.

Only a month later, the Court approved by six to three the promotion of a woman over a man who had scored a few points higher in a qualifying interview. With this decision, said one national-affairs publication, the Court "laid to rest the last remaining doubts about its endorsement of limited preferential treatment for women and minorities to remedy the effects of past discrimination in the work place."

But, said the Court in two other decisions of 1984 and 1986, white employees under a seniority system may not be laid off to protect the jobs of black workers hired under an affirmative action plan.

"Congress intended to protect from discrimination identifiable classes of persons who are subjected to intentional discrimination solely because of their ancestry or ethnic characteristics." These were the words of Justice White in 1987, writing for a unanimous Court, in ruling that the Civil Rights Act of 1866 and other federal civil rights protections may be used to prevent discrimination against ethnic groups such as Jews and Arabs, as well as against other minority groups and women.

ILLEGITIMATE CHILDREN are entitled to equal protection under the Constitution, the Court held in 1974, and struck down a section of the Social Security Act that denied benefits to some of them. From 1900 to 1969, the Court heard only six cases on the status of illegitimate children; since then it has heard more than twenty.

Most state and federal statutes governing legal relations between men and women and their offspring have long been based on conventional forms of marriage and divorce. But as the 1980's began, hundreds of thousands of couples were choosing to live together outside of marriage, sometimes raising families and staying together over long periods of time.

Adopted children, now grown, are challenging state laws that have sealed their birth records, thus preventing them from learning the identity of their natural parents. Husbands are demanding alimony from wives, and in 1979 the Supreme Court struck down a state law that denied support payments from wife to husband. Some childless couples are contracting with "surrogate mothers" to provide them with babies, leading to complex custody and paternity battles. Unmarried partners who have separated are suing for support and custody of children. "Palimony" suits are being brought by disappointed partners seeking damages or shares of property.

In other areas, too, the limits of constitutional protection are yet to be determined. Some people seek to apply traditional standards to new situations. Are privately owned shopping malls subject to free speech requirements as old-fashioned Main Streets are? In one case the answer was a qualified yes; in another, a qualified no. Are religious groups free, under the First Amendment, to distribute literature other than in designated locations in state fairgrounds in disregard of rules applied to all exhibitors? The Court said no in 1981.

Legal scholars observe that the Court's docket is changing markedly as new issues arise. Among them are the rights of the handicapped, the elderly, minors, illegal aliens and their children, homosexuals, students and teachers; experiments with preferential treatment for minority businesses; immunity of a government employee when acting in an official capacity; freedom-of-information laws as they are applied to intelligence and security agencies of the government; television in the courtroom; and the constitutionality of laws prohibiting the sale of drug paraphernalia.

Other questions touch subjects that were

NEW FORM OF LIFE *(below), developed in a laboratory, raises new legal questions. Denied a patent for a genetically engineered bacterium that can break down components of crude oil, Dr. Ananda M. Chakrabarty (opposite) appealed to the Supreme Court. In 1980 the high tribunal said that Chakrabarty's discovery "is not nature's handiwork, but his own; accordingly it is patentable subject matter"* **(Diamond v. Chakrabarty).** *Existing patent laws, the Court ruled, protect Chakrabarty's rights as an inventor.*

As scientific frontiers expand and social changes accelerate, the Supreme Court will continue to interpret the Nation's basic law.

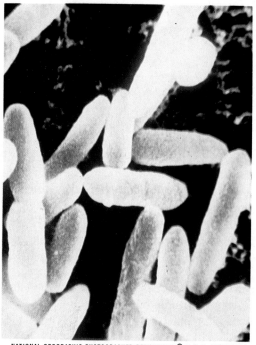

reserved to science fiction not long ago. In 1980 the Court was called upon to decide whether a new form of life, created from a combination of inanimate components, could be patented. Eight years earlier a microbiologist, Ananda M. Chakrabarty of Schenectady, New York, had developed a bacterium capable of breaking down several components of crude oil. Naturally occurring bacteria were able to degrade only one component. Chakrabarty's organism was a product of genetic engineering, capable of mass production, and promised among its benefits more efficient and rapid control of destructive oil spills.

By a five-to-four vote, the Court held that Chakrabarty's discovery represented a new and man-made form of life; that it constituted a "manufacture" or "composition of matter" as defined by the patent laws originally drafted by Thomas Jefferson; and that Chakrabarty's rights as an inventor were entitled to protection. Warnings of hazards from genetic research were brushed aside by the opinion; these considerations, said the Court, should be presented to Congress.

AS AMERICANS PENETRATE the finite and reach ever farther into the infinity of space, as their political, economic, and social institutions take new forms, their Constitution will be the final arbiter of their liberties and obligations. So long as the Supreme Court remains the voice of the Constitution, it will have to say what the law is. This is "the very essence of judicial duty," by John Marshall's own definition. Other citizens will have to speak, with the Justices, to defend the principle James Madison proclaimed: "While we assert for ourselves a freedom . . . we cannot deny an equal freedom to those whose minds have not yet yielded to the evidence which has convinced us."

For the Supreme Court alone cannot sustain our heritage of equal justice under law. Although the Court symbolizes the judicial power of the United States in action, it shares its highest duty with everyone who loves liberty. And, as Abraham Lincoln asked in 1861, "Why should there not be a patient confidence in the ultimate justice of the people?"

Within the Court Today

"I THOUGHT they would, well, talk Latin or something." The visitor had heard argument at the Supreme Court for the first time. On another occasion, a high-school girl reported "shock" that a black-robed Justice would rock in his high-backed chair and actually laugh out loud.

Chief Justice William H. Rehnquist first observed the Court's unchanging ritual opening when he was a newly hired law clerk in 1952, and in a recent book described it as a "stirring ceremony." No other regularly scheduled occasion guarantees a visitor "a view of so many persons responsible for the functioning of one of the three branches of the United States government."

To its majestic setting and moments of sheer ritual, the Supreme Court brings its distinctive manner of working in public—by listening to one lawyer at a time and asking tough questions. Its atmosphere mingles informality with dramatic tension. In a city of bureaucracy, it keeps the directness of a group of nine. It cherishes its courtesies.

Tour guides trained by the Curator's Office convey this mood when they talk about the Chamber to members of the public. No, there's no jury; there are no witnesses; the Justices don't need them because they review a printed record of what happened in some other court.

The guide calls attention to the sculptured marble frieze overhead; to the right, on the south wall, great lawgivers of the pre-Christian era; to the left, those of Christian times. A note of pride enters her voice as she indicates the panel over the main entrance, the one the Justices face: Powers of Evil—Corruption, Deceit—offset by Powers of Good—Security, Charity, Peace, with Justice flanked by Wisdom and Truth.

"The Republic endures and this is the symbol of its faith." So spoke Chief Justice Charles Evans Hughes on October 13, 1932, at a ceremony in which he joined President Herbert Hoover in laying the cornerstone of the new Supreme Court Building. In those days many had cause to doubt his words; since 1929 the country had been sinking deeper into the Great Depression.

Five months later the Chief Justice administered the Presidential oath to Franklin Delano Roosevelt. By October 7, 1935, when the Supreme Court convened for the first time in its new home, the national mood was less desperate.

Nations and empires have vanished since those days; but the Republic, though embattled or distraught in a tumultuous world, has endured. So has its faith, a stubborn one. So has the Supreme Court, surviving its epic collision with FDR and more than one onslaught in recent years.

Gleaming bone white and austere among its distinguished neighbors on Capitol Hill, its stately facade evoking the long-enduring glory of ancient Rome, the Supreme Court Building imposes a mood of decorum. Nothing less than a bedrock issue such as *U. S.* v. *Nixon* or the question of the death penalty brings out spectators to crowd the white plaza before it—and even then the sense of order strikes observers.

That aura of formality is no accident.

When architect Cass Gilbert submitted his design in May, 1929, he planned "a building of dignity and importance suitable . . . for the permanent home of the Supreme Court of the United States." Gilbert had been chosen by a commission led by Chief Justice William Howard Taft. Gilbert's associates were Cass Gilbert, Jr., and John R. Rockart, with executive supervision by David Lynn, Architect of the Capitol.

THE COURT'S TOUR DIRECTOR, *Priscilla Goodwin, explains details of the Courtroom to visitors— from the Justices' chairs of various styles to the ornamental ceiling. In a frieze above the bench, the central figures symbolize the power of government and the majesty of law. Courtroom lectures, given by the Curator's Office on a regular schedule, are open to the public.*

IDEALIZED IN BRONZE: *the Court's bench, which was angled in 1972.*

SCULPTURE BY PHILLIP RATNER; WIDTH 43 INCHES

COURTROOM ATTENDANTS *of the October
1987 term, supervised by Chief Deputy Marshal
Charles E. Cornelison, prepare the Chamber
for a public session. The attendants, sometimes
prelaw or night law-school students, deliver
messages to the Justices, go for books from the
library, and run other errands while the Court
is in session. Cards on counsel's tables explain
Courtroom procedure.*

*Either the Marshal or his deputy acts as
Crier, formally opening each session. Gavel
in hand, Marshal Alfred Wong intones the
centuries-old "Oyez!"—pronounced "o-yay,"
and meaning "Hear ye!"*

Into the building the architects put about three million dollars' worth of marble. For the exterior walls alone a thousand freight-car loads of flawless stone came from Vermont—along with a 250-ton slab specifically cut for sculptor James E. Fraser's allegorical figures at the entrance.

Georgia marble was chosen for the outer walls of four courtyards that divide the building into a cross-shaped center core and a gallery of offices and corridors. Nearly square, the resulting structure is 92 feet high and stretches 385 feet on its longest side. The interior walls are faced with marble quarried in Alabama.

Opposite the formal entrance, at the east end of the aptly named Great Hall, is the Court Chamber proper—82 by 91 feet, with a coffered ceiling 44 feet high. Gilbert walled this imposing room with Ivory Vein marble from Spain. For the 24 massive columns he insisted on marble of a particularly delicate tint, called Light Siena, from the Old Convent quarry in the Italian province of Liguria.

From Italy the rough stone went to a firm of marble finishers in Knoxville, Tennessee, who dressed and honed the blocks into 72 slightly tapered cylinders, 11 feet in circumference at the widest. Three sections went into each 30-foot column, to be topped by an Ionic capital.

Darker marble from Italy and Africa gives color to the floor. Against the marble the room gains richness from its fittings: tones of red in carpet and upholstery and heavy draperies, highly polished luster in solid Honduras mahogany, gleaming bronze latticework in gates to the side corridors. And in 1973, new lighting, new paint, and new gilding restored the ornamented ceiling to a brilliance time had dimmed since its installation nearly 40 years before.

Congress had authorized $9,740,000 for the construction and equipment of the building. When the project was reported finished on June 22, 1939, it had cost $93,532.02 less than the authorized amount.

Neither Taft nor the architect lived to see their dream building completed. Taft died in 1930, Gilbert four years later.

Not everyone liked the new building. Associate Justice Harlan Fiske Stone, who later became Chief, at first called it "almost bombastically pretentious . . . wholly inappropriate for a quiet group of old boys such as the Supreme Court." One of the old boys reportedly said that he and his brethren would be "nine black beetles in the Temple of Karnak." Another—undoubtedly thinking of exotic pomp rather than domestic party symbols—remarked that the Justices ought to enter it riding on elephants.

Such comments suggest how different men have regarded their own remarkable positions of power, prestige, and responsibility in the life of the Nation. Off the bench their successors show a similar concern—how to maintain a sense of human perspective in their marble temple.

The President appoints Justices with the advice and consent of the Senate, which takes its duty soberly. Since 1789 the Senate has rejected roughly one out of five formal nominations and has argued others at length. For a solid reason: As one Justice says, "Once we're here, they can't fire us."

Article III of the Constitution provides that the Justices, and all other federal judges, hold their offices "during good Behaviour." (And while they serve, their pay cannot be cut.) They may resign at any time, or retire when eligible. Once confirmed, however, they may be removed—in accordance with Article II—only by "Impeachment for, and Conviction of, Treason, Bribery, or other

TRIUMPHS OF MANKIND *in developing a just society blazon the bronze doors of the main west entrance. Eight relief panels trace the growth of law from ancient Greece and Rome to the young United States. Each door weighs 6½ tons, and slides into a wall recess when opened. Tortoises (left), perhaps representing the deliberate pace of the law, support bronze lamp standards in the foyer.*

REPORTER OF DECISIONS *Frank D. Wagner writes summaries of opinions and supervises publication of the record of the Court's work.*

high Crimes and Misdemeanors." In effect, they serve for life. Never in the Nation's history has a Supreme Court Justice been removed by impeachment.

When he or she takes the oath to uphold the Constitution and dons a robe, a Justice can enjoy an almost Olympian detachment. Members of the Court find it prudent to keep relationships with legislators and Presidents cordial but at arm's length. The Chief Justice, however, does confer with them on matters of judicial administration. The Court's budget must be supported before Congress, and codes of judicial conduct urge Justices to express their views on matters affecting the judicial system.

But by the very nature of the position, a Justice escapes some of the pressures and tensions that vex many public servants and take so much of their time: the orders or requests from other officials, the demands of constituents, the tactful or ham-handed approaches from lobbyists.

At the Court the strongest pressure takes a subtle form, felt in the mind or conscience.

Senior Associate Justice William J. Brennan, Jr., has defined it as the awareness of fallible human beings "that their best may not be equal to the challenge."

A single close case exerts its pressure. A rising caseload heightens it. The pressure makes for an air of aloofness, but that is part discipline, part illusion.

FORMALITY in the Courtroom and in the published opinion pays homage to tradition; but a custom of two centuries' standing was quietly ended on November 14, 1980. The Justices decided to drop the "Mr." in front of "Justice," which until that time had been used in published opinions and official records for 190 years.

When, almost a year later, Sandra Day O'Connor became the first woman to sit on the high bench, the new usage was already established, and "Justice O'Connor" was a natural way to address her. But most attorneys addressing the bench still open their remarks with the familiar "Mr. Chief Justice."

Formality, courtesy, and dignity are not empty custom; they are vital to colleagues who are compelled to disagree publicly in print, expressing their deepest convictions, but always respecting the equally deep convictions of their fellow Justices.

By statute, the annual term begins the first Monday in October. By custom, it ends when the year's schedule of cases is finished. Spring brings the notorious end-of-term crunch. Justice Brennan tells of taking up a heated end-of-term disagreement with Justice Hugo Black, who said of the season: "This place can become like a pressure cooker and it can beat the strongest of men."

Most of the Justices can be found in their chambers on Saturdays throughout the term, and frequently on Sundays. Even in summer, after the Justices have wound up the formal schedule, new petitions follow them at the rate of a hundred a week; motions such as those for stays of judgment must be dealt with; and appeals of national significance may bring the Court back into session.

In reality their duties never end, and during the 1978-79 term the Court reluctantly recognized that the recess had become a fiction and began letting each term run until the new one opened.

MORE THAN 300 PEOPLE work regularly in the Supreme Court Building. Among them are the principal officers appointed by the Court to ensure the proper execution of its complex statutory duties: the Clerk, the Reporter of Decisions, the Librarian, and the Marshal.

For all judicial matters, the Clerk, Joseph F. Spaniol, Jr., his chief deputy, Francis J. Lorson, and their staff of 26 are the link between the Justices and the legal world outside. They handle a rising flow of paper work, preparing the Court's calendar as they check, record, and sort the incoming cases for presentation.

In 1941-42 the Court had 1,302 docketed cases; by the end of the 1980 term, the number had grown to 5,144, and the annual inflow remains near that level. From these, only 150 to 180 are taken up for oral argument. In 1975 the Court placed the Clerk's records on a computer, but every motion

and thousands of briefs must still be carefully processed by hand.

To deal with this fourfold increase in work and to prevent enormous backlogs, the Court has increased staff size and productivity to a point many consider the limit. Chief Justice William H. Rehnquist talks with repugnance of the possibility that any case might receive "anything less than the best attention from any one of the nine."

Of the 1980 filings, about half came *in forma pauperis*, from people unable to pay the costs. Of such cases, about a quarter are from prison inmates who claim some violation of rights. One of the Clerk's staff pulls samples from a shelf in a room full of bulky files. "I received a sentence of death for first degree murder and am presently in custody on Death Row at Florida State Prison," a petitioner writes. For his limited part in a robbery conspiracy involving killing, he pleads, the death penalty would be cruel and unusual

MUCH ADMIRED BUT SELDOM USED *stairs spiral through five floors. Two elliptical staircases, closed to the public, fascinate visitors. Despite such showpieces, the building cost nearly $94,000 less than the $9,740,000 appropriated for it.*

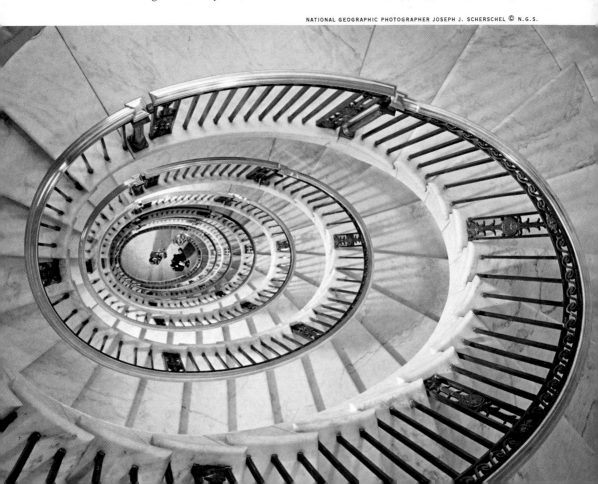

punishment, in violation of the Eighth Amendment. In another petition, an indigent woman in Texas, seeking to establish the fatherhood of her son, challenges the constitutionality of a state law that says paternity suits must be brought before the child is one year old.

The Clerk of the Court's staff separates such cases from the paid ones, noting in passing the changes in the types of filings: "Now we're getting many discrimination and affirmative action cases, appeals involving political contributions, family law cases, First Amendment cases, and always appeals of criminal convictions."

The Clerk also receives lawyers' applications for admission to the Supreme Court bar—some 5,000 a year. The number jumped suddenly to 12,000 in 1979, just before an increase in the fee from $25 to $100. The Clerk schedules the introduction of candidates who wish to appear in person. After the Chief Justice has greeted them before the bench, the Clerk swears them in as members of this bar; only a few ever appear again. More than 172,000 lawyers have been admitted since 1925.

Alfred Wong, the Marshal since 1976, is responsible for financial matters, including payrolls and bills, and for supplies. The Marshal coordinates ceremonies—memorial services for deceased Justices, investitures of new Justices. He directs the Court's police force. He arranges the reception of dignitaries and other visitors, and he is the building superintendent.

Visitors are invited to view the Courtroom at any time when the Court is not in session; brief lectures are given there every hour on the half hour. On the ground floor the public may see two graceful spiral staircases and the

SHRINE AND SEAT OF JUSTICE, *the Court's first permanent home welcomes visitors at the rate of more than 800,000 annually. Sightseers in the Great Hall stroll past marble busts of the Chief Justices. Above, workmen on scaffolds repaint the ceiling of the hall in June, 1974, its first renewal since the building opened in 1935.*

IN THE MAIN READING ROOM *of the third-floor library, paneled in handcarved oak, attorneys and*

Justices' clerks tap a reference collection of more than 250,000 lawbooks, records, and journals.

CURATOR GAIL GALLOWAY *(right) and
Assistant Curator Marguerite Glass-Englehart
organize documents and memorabilia for
an exhibit celebrating the bicentennial
of the Constitution. The Curators supervise
the Court's historical collections.*

cases, on Monday through Wednesday, with two weeks of recess, for opinion-writing.

Spectators are admitted to the Chamber as seats become available. The public seating capacity is 218, and 55 places can be added; but for the most dramatic cases and special occasions there is never enough room.

All visitors must check coats, briefcases, umbrellas, and cameras before entering the Chamber. Marshal Wong and his aides may politely find clothes too informal. Standards have relaxed greatly since coats and ties were obligatory for men, but T-shirts, slacks, and

historical exhibits that are among the responsibilities of the Curator, Gail Galloway. In 1982 this area acquired a magnificent centerpiece: a larger-than-life bronze statue of John Marshall. It had stood on the west terrace of the Capitol since 1884, when the Supreme Court still met in that building.

Since 1970, burgundy carpeting and green plants in the corridors and flowers in the courtyards have relieved the austerity of the marble. Gold and deep red then replaced institutional green in the cafeteria, which is open to the public but reserves special time at lunch for the Court staff in the interest of efficiency. A snack bar provides additional food service.

The Court is increasingly popular among visitors to Washington, and the number who came to look and listen reached 800,000 in 1987. Visitors who want to see the Court at work should check its schedule in advance. Usually it alternates two weeks of hearing

shoes are the very minimum required for admittance. The presence of small children is not encouraged—"Oh, no younger than about six," says a police officer. "But the young ones usually behave; they seem to catch the atmosphere."

Constantly during a session the aisles are patrolled to see that no one breaks the rules by writing or sketching (permitted only in the press section) or whispering or, as officially described, expressing "favor or disfavor." Even draping one's arm over the back of a chair is still against the rules of decorum but, as Marshal Wong says with a chuckle, "We no longer insist that attorneys in the bar section keep their suit coats buttoned."

In another break with venerable practice, beginning in 1973 the system of choosing

STATUE OF JOHN MARSHALL *presides over the Lower Great Hall in the Supreme Court building. Quotations from the Chief Justice's opinions, incised on a backdrop of Alabama marble, honor his 34 years on the Court and complement an exhibit commemorating the Constitution.*

high-school freshmen as Court pages was gradually discontinued. Now there are Courtroom attendants, slightly older and sometimes chosen from the ranks of prelaw and night law-school students.

While the Court is in session, the attendants wait on small straight chairs behind the bench. They move swiftly to pass notes from Justices to others in the Court. They may disappear behind the red draperies to deliver a message, to fill a water glass at one of two fountains on the rear wall, or to obtain reference material from the library. They may have unusual errands, as Justice Harry A. Blackmun recalls from his first day on the bench—June 9, 1970:

"I had taken my seat, and was examining things. I pulled open a drawer in the bench, and found some cough drops. And a copy of the Constitution, stamped 'O. W. Holmes' and signed by Justice Frankfurter, a successor in this seat. The Marshal brought me a Bible to sign—presented by the first Justice Harlan and signed by all the Justices since. Suddenly Byron White was leaning over to me, whispering. 'Harry! Harry, where's your spittoon?' He snapped a finger—softly—for a page. *'Get the Justice his spittoon!'*"

Today the spittoons serve as wastepaper baskets. Before each chair at the four counsel tables lie white goose-quill pens, neatly crossed; most lawyers appear before the Court only once, and gladly take the quills home as souvenirs. Snuffboxes, once indispensable, vanished long ago, along with arguments that lasted for hours and soared to splendid heights of oratory.

OPENING FORMALITIES link the current day to the past. The Marshal or Deputy Marshal acts as Crier. A few minutes before 10 a.m., Crier and Clerk, formally dressed in cutaways, go to their desks below the ends of the high bench. Pencils, pens, papers, briefs, and a pewter mug of water are at each Justice's place.

At their tables, attorneys glance over notes or confer softly. A young lawyer may fidget slightly, while a veteran checks his watch. Seconds will count, for today each counsel has only 30 minutes—unless he or she has a very unusual case.

Meanwhile, the Justices, summoned by buzzer, gather in their conference room. Each shakes hands with all the others, even if they were chatting a few minutes earlier. Chief Justice Fuller instituted this unvarying custom as a sign that "harmony of aims if not views is the Court's guiding principle."

Promptly at 10 o'clock the Crier brings down his gavel. Everyone rises instantly as he intones: "The Honorable, the Chief Justice and the Associate Justices of the Supreme Court of the United States!"

As the Crier speaks, the nine Justices stride through openings in the curtains and move to their places. The Crier chants his call for silence: "Oyez! Oyez!! Oyez!!!" From the centuries that Anglo-Norman or "law French" was the language of English courts, the word for "Hear ye!" survives.

Steady-voiced, the Crier continues: "All persons having business before the Honorable, the Supreme Court of the United States, are admonished to draw near and give their attention, for the Court is now sitting. God save the United States and this Honorable Court!"

The gavel falls again. The Justices and all others take their seats. Visitors unacquainted with the Court can quickly check identifications against seating charts.

In the center sits Chief Justice Rehnquist, who began his Supreme Court career more than 35 years ago as a law clerk. Born in Milwaukee, a lawyer in Phoenix for 16 years, William Rehnquist came back to Washington as Assistant Attorney General in 1969, and was named to the Supreme Court as an Associate Justice in 1972. Appointed Chief Justice by President Reagan, he was sworn in on September 26, 1986.

Seniority determines the seating of the eight Associate Justices, alternating between the Chief's right and his left.

INNER COURTYARD, *one of four, offers a springtime setting for a midday break enjoyed by law clerks and secretaries, messengers and other staff members, with snacks available to them from facilities on the ground floor. "You see," says one of the Court's staff, "this place is something more than nine overpowering presences."*

SENIOR ASSOCIATE JUSTICE *William J. Brennan, Jr., closely reviews an attorney's brief.*
A New Jersey state judge before his appointment by President Eisenhower in 1956, Brennan
has served on the Court longer than any other present Justice. A stalwart defender of the
Bill of Rights, he believes that "From its founding, the Nation's basic commitment has been
to foster the dignity and well-being of all persons within its borders."

At his immediate right sits the senior Associate, William Joseph Brennan, Jr., who ascended the ranks of the New Jersey court system, from trial judge to Associate Justice of the state's highest court. He served for more than three years in the Army in World War II, leaving as a colonel. A Democrat, Brennan was appointed to the Court by Republican President Eisenhower in 1956.

At the Chief's immediate left sits Byron Raymond White of Colorado, onetime Rhodes scholar and All-American football player, Deputy Attorney General from January, 1961, until appointed to the Court in 1962 by President Kennedy.

To Brennan's right:

Thurgood Marshall, born in Baltimore, longtime attorney for the NAACP, judge of the Court of Appeals for the Second Circuit from 1961 to 1965, Solicitor General from 1965 to 1967, named to the Court by President Lyndon B. Johnson in 1967.

John Paul Stevens, Chicagoan, in the Navy during World War II, then in private practice for more than 20 years, appointed to the U. S. Court of Appeals for the Seventh Circuit in 1970, placed on the Supreme Court by President Ford in 1975.

Antonin Scalia, native of Trenton, N.J., graduate of Harvard Law School, in private practice from 1962 to 1967, professor of law, Assistant Attorney General from 1974 to 1977, appointed judge of the United States Court of Appeals for the District of Columbia Circuit in 1982, elevated to the Supreme Court in 1986 by President Reagan.

From Chief Justice Rehnquist's left, after Justice White:

Harry A. Blackmun, in practice in Minnesota for 16 years, general counsel to the Mayo medical organizations for almost a decade, judge of the Eighth Circuit Court of Appeals from 1959 to 1970, when he was named to this Court by President Nixon.

Sandra Day O'Connor, born in Texas, in private practice in Arizona from 1959 to 1965, Assistant Attorney General of Arizona for the next four years, a state senator from 1969 to 1975, trial court judge and then judge of the Arizona Court of Appeals until she was appointed to the Supreme Court by President Reagan in 1981.

Anthony M. Kennedy, from California,

COURT'S OWN LEGAL OFFICE, *created in 1973, helps the Justices and the Court staff deal with the hundreds of special motions, applications, and petitions—some requiring decisions within hours—that reach the Court each term. Here, Staff Counsel William Dennis McKinnie (left) indicates a key paragraph in a discussion with Counsel Richard G. R. Schickele.*

OLD GLORY LOOKS LIKE NEW *after seamstress Odessa I. White repairs a tear in a flag flown before the Supreme Court Building. Justices' robes and police uniforms also receive her special care. Pfc. James D. Kendrick (left) makes notes as he talks with Chief Kenneth F. Conlon; behind them, Edward L. Turner, Jr., of the Clerk's office, confers with Pfc. Lisa A. Spindler and Pfc. Francis J. Kehoe. From the control panel, Kendrick can reach security police stationed throughout the Court building. The public may visit the building from 9 to 4:30, Monday through Friday.*

graduate of Harvard Law School, in private practice from 1962 to 1975, professor of constitutional law since 1965, judge of the Ninth Circuit Court of Appeals from 1975 until his appointment to this Court by President Reagan was confirmed in 1988.

Argument is easier for all to follow since the Justices approved a change in the shape of their bench. "I remember when I used to argue cases here," a senior lawyer recalls. "I would get two questions at once, from opposite ends of the bench—the Justices couldn't see or hear each other." In 1972 the bench was altered to its present shape, with two wings each set at an 18-degree angle, a form that has been widely used in American courts since the mid-1950's.

Even the technical cases can stir alert attention as the lawyer begins—"Mr. Chief Justice, and may it please the Court . . ."—and develops his theme—" . . . insurance companies are entitled to justice like anybody else. . . ." The questions start: brisk, no-nonsense queries from Justice O'Connor; gentle but probing questions from Justice Brennan; a low-pitched inquiry from Chief Justice Rehnquist.

A touch of humor sometimes enlivens an exchange and brings a subdued ripple of laughter. Justice White, onetime professional football halfback, rocking in his chair as he listens to an attorney arguing Presidential immunity, suddenly leans forward

when he hears the term "blind-sided." "Is that a term of art?" he asks.

An attorney used to this Court may take an unwelcome idea in stride: "Possibly, your Honor, but I would suggest. . . ." Or suavely field a question on what Congress intended in a statute: ". . . the Congress does many things that I wonder at. . . ."

With veiled ruefulness a lawyer remarks, "I see my time is running short"; or the Chief Justice may offer a gentle reminder, "Counsel, you are now using up your rebuttal time." Or the other way around: "We have taken much of your time with our questions; we will give you six more minutes."

When a red light glows on the lectern, the Chief Justice says, "Thank you, Counsel. The case is submitted."

SUPREME COURT cases come in three varieties. Least numerous are the "original jurisdiction" actions, brought by one state against another, or between states and the federal government. The Constitution

TWICE A WEEK *during the regular term, the Justices meet in the conference room above. A consensus of four brings a case up for review. Forging the majority needed for a final decision can be hard when a vacancy exists on the bench—most recently when President Reagan's first two nominees to the Court failed to gain Senate approval.*

Officers of the Supreme Court (right) meet each month under the direction of Noel J. Augustyn, Administrative Assistant to the Chief Justice. From left: Clerk Joseph F. Spaniol, Jr.; Cyril A. Donnelly, Director of Budget and Personnel; Librarian Stephen G. Margeton; Reporter of Decisions Frank D. Wagner; Counsel Richard G. R. Schickele; Mr. Augustyn; James R. Donovan, Director of Data Systems; Marshal Alfred Wong; Public Information Officer Toni House; Curator Gail Galloway.

also empowers the Court to hear "all Cases affecting Ambassadors, other public Ministers and Consuls." In these the Court sits as a trial body from which there is no appeal.

Few original jurisdiction cases are filed—usually one to five a term—but sheer bulk makes many of these difficult.

In 1952 Arizona sued California over water from the Colorado River. The completed trial record covered more than 26,000 pages. Briefs and other documents filed by the states took 4,000 more. The Justices heard 16 hours of oral argument in the fall of 1961, six hours more in November, 1962. Arizona prevailed in the Court's decision in 1963.

More numerous, but mercifully shorter, are cases from state courts. If any state tribunal decides a federal question and the

FROM COURTROOM VIA PRESSROOM, *cases reach the public. Within seconds of the announcement of a decision, a phone call from the Clerk's office notifies information officer Toni House, who distributes copies of each new opinion to assembled reporters. Official documents bear the Court's seal, shown on a bar admission certificate, imprinted by Assistant Clerk Calvin Todd.*

litigant has no further remedy within the state, the Supreme Court may consider it.

Most common—roughly two-thirds of the total—are requests for review of decisions of federal appellate or district courts. The great majority of cases reach the Supreme Court through its granting of petitions for writs of certiorari, from the Latin *certiorari volumus,* "we wish to be informed."

Normally the "writ of cert" says in effect to an appellate court, "Send us the record in this case you decided recently." In very rare instances a writ of certiorari before appellate judgment says, "Send us the record in this case you haven't reviewed yet." It enables the Court to act with maximum speed in unusual cases of great public importance.

With more than 5,000 petitions annually, deciding which cases to decide is a load in itself. According to a court historian,

"it is arguably the most important stage in the entire Supreme Court process."

EACH JUSTICE determines how he or she will vote on each certiorari petition, usually calling for a law clerk's memorandum detailing the petition. Since 1972 several of the Justices have used a "cert pool" system. As the certiorari petitions are received, their clerks take turns writing memorandums. These are distributed to the Justices in the pool—currently Rehnquist, White, Blackmun, O'Connor, and Scalia—and each conducts whatever additional research is necessary. The other Justices prefer to rely on their own clerks, but all the Justices review all petitions.

Roughly 70 percent of the petitions end at this point, with a vote not to accept the case. The Justices may be satisfied that the decision of the lower court was correct, or that the case has no national significance, or, in some instances, that the Supreme Court lacks jurisdiction. Whatever the reason for denial, the effect is to allow the decision of the lower court to stand.

Of the cases remaining, the Justices screen the problems closely—by a process that they explain freely in outline. They meet on Wednesdays and Fridays during the term in a conference room as secret as any in the government. In a capital full of classified matters, and full of leaks, the Court keeps private matters private. Reporters may speculate; but details of discussion are never disclosed, and the vote is

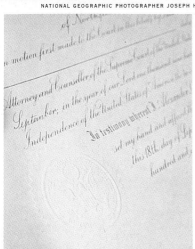

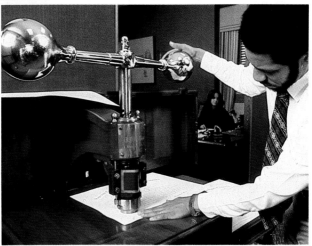

revealed only when a decision is announced.

No outsider enters the room during conference. The junior Associate acts as "doorkeeper," sending for reference material, for instance, and receiving it at the door.

"We could not function as a court if our conferences were public," Justice Blackmun said in an interview. "There are just the nine of us, no more. . . . [W]e can say what we initially believe, only to be proved wrong by the honing effect of conference and agreement and disagreement."

Five minutes before conference time, 9:30 or 10 a.m., a buzzer summons the Justices. They exchange ritual handshakes and settle down at the long table. The Chief sits at the east end; the other Justices sit at places they have chosen in order of their seniority.

Before each Justice is a copy of the day's agenda. Each decides when he or she should refrain from taking any part in a case.

The Chief Justice opens the discussion, summarizing each case. The senior Associate speaks next, and comment passes down the line. To be accepted for review, a case needs only four votes, fewer than the majority required for a decision on the case itself. Counsel for the litigants are directed to submit their printed briefs so that each Justice has a set several weeks before argument.

PARADOXICALLY, PERHAPS—in light of the complete confidentiality of the conference—the Supreme Court is one of the most open of government agencies and one of the most public of courts. It acts only on matters of public record; it hears counsel's arguments in public; all its orders and opinions are on the record; all materials presented to the Court for reaching its decisions are available to the public. All conference decisions are published. The disagreements among the Justices are fully exposed to the public in the written opinions, and on occasion the language of dissent becomes vehement. Justice Blackmun explains, ". . . these are strongminded individuals. . . . [T]hey entertain their positions strongly . . . they believe in them. . . ."

News representatives are fully informed of what cases are brought before the Court and may consult all the records. They may obtain summaries of cases accepted for review well before they are heard; the summaries are prepared by law professors throughout the country. When decisions are announced from the bench, a special telephone carries word to the newsroom to distribute the printed opinions immediately.

When the vote has been taken on a case, the writing of an opinion is assigned—by the Chief if he voted with the majority, otherwise by the senior Justice of the majority. Dissenters may agree among themselves on who will explain their view. Any Justice, concurring or dissenting, may write an individual opinion to emphasize a special point.

As drafting begins, the law clerks intensify their search for pertinent material. They work very hard, says Chief Justice Rehnquist, and after an arduous 12-month stint "are glad to go on to something else in the profession." They come to the Court as top graduates of law schools, alert to current research and thinking there. Appointment as a clerk carries great honor.

Justice White was clerk to the late Chief Justice Vinson; Chief Justice Rehnquist was clerk to the late Justice Jackson; Justice Stevens's first service at the Court was as clerk to the late Justice Rutledge. Then each Justice had two clerks, a secretary, and a messenger; today each may have four clerks and two secretaries, as well as a messenger.

A Justice in need of additional legal or historical references, or information of any kind, has the help of Stephen G. Margeton, Librarian and Officer of the Court, and his staff of 24. They consult a collection of more than 250,000 volumes, very close to the shelf capacity of the beautiful oak-paneled library. Like other parts of the Court, the library has taken advantage of modern technology, using microfilm to save space and enlarge the collection and computerized data banks to extend its reach. At their terminals, library researchers can tap almost instantly into both general and more specialized remote sources of information.

Professional writers themselves, Justices spend hours and days of painstaking work on draft opinions. When an author is satisfied with a document, it is circulated for the reactions of colleagues. When these comments come in, he or she often finds that the work has just begun.

SANDRA DAY O'CONNOR *(below)*
with her hand on a family Bible
held by her husband, John,
repeats an oath to uphold the
Constitution, administered by
Chief Justice Warren Burger in
the Justices' Conference Room.
On September 25, 1981, Justice
O'Connor became the first
woman to serve on the Supreme
Court, thus fulfilling a campaign
promise made by Ronald Reagan
to place a woman on the Nation's
highest tribunal.

Five years later, a new Chief
Justice, William H. Rehnquist
(far right), an Associate Justice
since 1972, and a new Associate
Justice, Antonin Scalia (near
right), leave the Court to meet
the public and the press. Along
with retiring Chief Justice Burger,
they descend the 36 marble steps
leading to Supreme Court Plaza.

In a rare published comment, Justice Brennan told of how he once "circulated 10 printed drafts before one was approved as the Court opinion." At the same time, dissenters are circulating their own drafts. "It is a common experience that dissents change votes, even enough votes to become the majority," Justice Brennan said.

Special duties interrupt the routine. Each member of the Court is Circuit Justice of one or more of the 12 federal judicial circuits. A Circuit Justice may be called upon to issue or stay an injunction, to grant bail, to stay a scheduled execution.

But finally, when all the revisions and corrections are complete, a master proof of the opinion is authorized for printing. On the day

of release, final copies go to the Clerk for safekeeping and to the Reporter of Decisions, Frank D. Wagner. Both Mr. Wagner and his assistant, Thomas G. Oliver, are lawyers. They write headnotes—short analytical summaries of the opinions.

Since 1970 journalists have received the headnotes along with opinions, an invaluable aid especially for wire service and radio and television correspondents, who in the past often had to go through hundreds of pages of opinions in minutes or be late with their news flashes. At a more measured pace, the Reporter also supervises publication of *United States Reports*, the official record of the Court's work.

In the pressroom, reporters wait, swap-

JOSEPH H. BAILEY, LARRY D. KINNEY © N.G.S.

ping shop talk over coffee: "This time it'll be at least six to three, maybe seven to two . . ." "That will put the whole thing back with Congress . . ." "But there's a difference between illegal aliens and legal immigrants . . ." "I say it's protected speech under the First Amendment . . ."

Public information officer Toni House distributes copies of the decisions when word comes of their announcement from the bench. Some reporters scatter to phones or typewriters. Others prepare to go out to do a "stand-up" television report before a camera crew carefully positioned on the plaza to show the classic facade of the Court behind the speaker.

Proceedings in the Supreme Court have been moving at a brisker pace in recent years. Most lawyers are admitted in absentia to Court practice, releasing many hours in the Court's schedule. The time allotted for oral argument has been cut from two hours to one. In most cases, only short summaries of opinions are read from the bench. These changes have saved one and a half days of Court time a week.

Until 1969 there was not even a copying machine at the Court; the junior Justice needed strong light and good glasses to work from a blurry eighth-carbon copy of a draft. Later in the decision-making process, the opinions, still in draft, were set by Linotype in the Court's printing shop and distributed to the Justices. Redrafting and editing required laborious resetting of lines of lead type, readjustment of pages and footnotes, proofreading after proofreading.

Today the technical aspects of decision-making are fully automated, with substantial savings in time and effort. Each of the nine Justices has, in effect, an individual word-processing and printing system closed off from the other eight. But once work has reached the state where a Justice wants to make an opinion available to colleagues, it can be sent to their chambers and printed instantly simply by pressing the right buttons. Editing, typesetting, and proofing can all be accomplished in a few hours.

Some of the Justices work on the computer themselves, but not all. Justice Brennan recently agreed that "the way we can process things now with all these new gadgets is wonderful, but . . . I have vowed I will never learn how to operate them. . . . I still handwrite everything."

JUSTICES AND THEIR SPOUSES *gather for a group portrait in the East Conference Room. From left:
standing, Justice and Mrs. Scalia, Justice Marshall, Justice and Mrs. Stevens, Justice Brennan,
Chief Justice Rehnquist, Justice White, Justice and Mr. O'Connor, Justice Blackmun, Mrs. and Justice
Kennedy; seated, Mrs. Marshall, Mrs. Brennan, Mrs. Rehnquist, Mrs. White, Mrs. Blackmun.*

THE CHIEF JUSTICE, as presiding officer of the Court, is responsible by statute for its administration, in addition to hearing cases and writing opinions. The duties of the Chief relating to the Court are spelled out in 20 paragraphs of the federal law, and range from assigning Associate Justices (and himself) to the circuits to approving regulations for the protection of the Court building and grounds. In practice, all matters affecting the Justices, procedures of the Court, and other weighty matters are discussed and sometimes voted in conference.

But the statutory duties of the Chief, spelled out in an additional 44 paragraphs of the federal code, extend far beyond the Court. He is responsible for the administrative leadership of the entire federal judicial system. He is chairman of the Judicial Conference of the United States, a "board of trustees" for the federal courts. He chairs the Federal Judicial Center, with its programs of research and education, and oversees the Administrative Office of the United States Courts, "housekeeper" and statistician for the federal court system.

The Chief Justice has an Administrative Assistant, Noel J. Augustyn, to help with these responsibilities. Television coverage, so important at the White House and Capitol, is not a concern. No official activity of the Court is open to television cameras.

By statute, the Chief Justice is on the boards of three cultural institutions—the National Gallery of Art, the Smithsonian Institution, and the Hirshhorn museum.

THE CROWDS BEGAN forming early at the Supreme Court plaza in the crystal sunlight of Friday, September 25, 1981. By 11 a.m. passersby knew a major event was in the offing; it looked as if all the news photographers in Washington had gathered there.

Precisely at noon, applause rippled through the crowds along the edges of the plaza as two black-robed figures came through the massive bronze doors in the shadow of the pillars of the Court building's west facade. Slowly descending the 36 marble steps, the two figures emerged suddenly into the sunshine, and the crowds could see the smiling faces of Chief Justice Burger and Sandra Day O'Connor, the first woman ever to be appointed to the Supreme Court. As they approached the cameras, they were joined by members of Justice O'Connor's family—her husband, Attorney John Jay O'Connor, their three grown sons, and the Justice's parents.

When Justice Stewart announced his retirement on June 18, 1981, speculation began at once over whether President Reagan would avail himself of this first opportunity to redeem a campaign pledge and appoint a woman, or await another vacancy.

The President ended the suspense in less than three weeks and announced his decision; he had chosen Sandra Day O'Connor, a 51-year-old judge on the Arizona Court of Appeals, a "person for all seasons."

The Senate Committee on the Judiciary held hearings on confirmation the week of September 7. For three days Senators probed her views on controversial issues, such as abortion, judicial "activism," and the Equal Rights Amendment. With tact, composure, and patience Judge O'Connor responded, but she refused to be drawn into prejudgments of issues likely to come before the Court. The Senate, with one member absent, confirmed her appointment 99 to 0.

At 2:12 p.m. on September 25, before a packed Courtroom, eight Justices appeared behind the high bench and took their places; Justice O'Connor, in street clothes, waited to one side. President and Mrs. Reagan watched from chairs below the bench as the new Justice came forward to take the oath.

"Justice O'Connor, welcome," Chief Justice Burger said simply when she had finished repeating the solemn words. Then, after donning her black robe, she took the chair assigned to her as the most junior member of America's most select and most prestigious judicial company.

The first Monday in October, opening day of the annual Court term, came only ten days later. Precisely at 10 a.m., the nine Justices took their places at the bench, and the Clerk intoned the ancient cry of "Oyez!" There was no alteration in the familiar routine, no sign that a tradition of almost two centuries had been broken. The membership of the Court had changed, but not the Court. It embodies the spirit of the people for whom it interprets the law of the land.

The Federal Court System

AMERICANS have long had a propensity for taking their grievances to court. Today this penchant for lawsuits has led to a "litigation explosion."

"People in this country insist on having resort to a judicial system, unlike other countries where they tend to use other means," notes Chief District Judge Aubrey E. Robinson, Jr. Contributing factors, he points out, are new federal programs and statutes of recent years—concerning civil rights, business practices, environmental protection—which bring more and more people into involvement with the law. Justice Blackmun concurs that perhaps the most important factor is the increasing amount of legislation "coming forth from Congress."

Case filings in the federal judicial system's 94 district trial courts more than doubled from 1960 to 1980. And in fiscal 1987 the district judges received 238,892 new civil cases—up some 70,000 from 1980. New criminal cases for 1987 totaled 43,292 compared with 28,932 in 1980.

The overload on the federal courts had already grown critical in the 1960's. In 1968 Congress provided some relief by creating a system of U. S. magistrates. In 1987 they handled more than 465,000 matters such as preliminary proceedings, pretrial conferences, and reports in certain civil cases and criminal misdemeanors. This gave judges more time for conducting trials.

Efforts to improve the efficiency and capacity of the federal judiciary were greatly intensified in the 1970's and 1980's through a series of initiatives by Chief Justice Burger. After 1971, each circuit could acquire a trained court executive officer for the administrative work that formerly fell on its chief judge. The Institute for Court Management, established in 1969, conducted 32 programs in 1985 attended by some 1,200 state and federal court officials; more than 440 people have completed an extensive Court Executive Development Program.

Juries with six members instead of twelve have been adopted by most of the district courts for civil, but not criminal, cases. Wide adoption of the "omnibus pretrial hearing," under which the contending parties in criminal cases must make all pretrial motions by an early fixed date, has reduced trial delays. Courts also are experimenting with various forms of alternative dispute resolution to expedite civil cases.

As a result of these and other measures, case dispositions for each trial judge increased from around 350 cases in 1979 to more than 530 in 1986. During the same period, the number of trial court judges rose from 516 to 575.

Case filings increased even faster. More than 200,000 cases were begun in 1981, one and a half times the number started in 1971. In comparison, in 1987 more than 280,000 new cases were filed, and some 268,000 were pending at the end of that fiscal year.

Cases appealed in the federal system also climbed dramatically. Between 1970 and 1980 they more than doubled. From 1979 to 1986 the number of appeals rose from 20,219 to 34,292—a 70 percent increase in only seven years. Measured over a longer period of 25 years, the number of appeals has grown more than six times as fast as the population.

In the 12 appeals circuits, the number of judges varies from 4 in the First to 23 in the Ninth Circuit. They work in panels of three on each case. In the ten years ending in 1981, pending cases rose from 286 to 490 a panel; by 1987 that figure had climbed to 699.

For most Americans and most cases, the Federal Court of Appeals is the end of the judicial road. "Of course, the Supreme Court can overrule us and all state courts as well," says Senior Judge George A. MacKinnon of the Federal Court of Appeals for the District of Columbia Circuit, "but in the world of hard reality we are nearly always the final court of review." He observed that of the more than 34,000 cases taken to the appeals courts in 1986, fewer than 200 will be heard by the Nation's highest tribunal.

Effective as they have been, there is an ultimate limit to procedural improvements.

No one wants apparent efficiency at the expense of justice for all. The painstaking techniques of courtroom questioning—techniques that John Marshall would find familiar and that are essential to a fair trial—simply cannot be hurried beyond built-in limits. Fair procedures and sound results count all the more in district courts because about 90 percent of all federal cases end there, without appeal.

Since 1968, both newly appointed and experienced judges, as well as court staffs, have had access to professional training by the Federal Judicial Center in Washington, D. C. Under the direction of John C. Godbold, the center trains almost 3,000 people each year—many in their home courts, others at the center's headquarters in Dolley Madison's old house on Lafayette Park.

Seminars for newly appointed judges ease a difficult transition. Experienced colleagues offer intensive lessons in how to manage complex civil cases or cope with unruly defendants, and how to adjust to new roles. "All of a sudden," says one new judge, "lawyer friends are afraid to ask you out to lunch."

A comparable institution, the National Center for State Courts, was established in 1971, and is now located in Williamsburg, Virginia. With Edward B. McConnell as Executive Director and a staff of more than 120 in six offices around the country, the center provides training programs, technical assistance, exchanges of information among the state judicial systems, and research—all aimed at improving the state courts.

More than 40 states have created State-Federal Judicial Councils in the last 20 years as a means of increasing cooperation and avoiding duplication. State courts may decide federal questions; federal courts must occasionally deal with state law; and a few cases such as multiple damage suits may be heard simultaneously in both state and

FISH STORY: *Finger-size snail darter (below) brought the giant Tellico Dam project to a standstill for more than two years. When the dam on the Little Tennessee River threatened the survival of the tiny fish, a species of perch, conservationists argued that the 1973 Endangered Species Act entitled it to protection. Holding that this was what Congress had mandated, the Court strictly enforced the law as written and said construction of the $137,000,000 project must stop. Congress then amended the law in order to complete the dam. Snail darters have since been found in other waters.*

TENNESSEE VALLEY AUTHORITY (BELOW) AND JIM ROBERTSON

Trial and Review

"I'LL TAKE THIS *to the Supreme Court!"*
*Furious, Bill Smith shouts this classic threat
at John Jones as they argue the blame for a
collision of Jones's expensive car and Smith's
heavily laden truck.*

*But to reach even the first rung of the
three-level federal court system, their quarrel
must qualify as a federal case. The Constitution
and Acts of Congress prescribe what matters
may come before U. S. courts. Others must
be tried in state courts.*

*If Smith and Jones live in different states—
and more than $10,000 is involved—a federal
district court can hear their dispute. Either
party, if unhappy with the outcome, may ask
review by a court of appeals.*

*Despite his angry promise, Smith in all
probability could take his case no further.*

*"No litigant is entitled to more than two
chances, namely, to the original trial and to
a review," Chief Justice William Howard Taft
told Congress in 1925. It wrote his view into
law with the "Judges' Bill."*

*To reach the Supreme Court, cases must
turn on principles of law, or constitutional
issues, of far-reaching importance. Of more
than 5,000 petitions a year, the highest court
accepts about 400—hearing argument on
perhaps 180, deciding the rest without debate.*

*Federal courts also review decisions of
administrative agencies such as the Federal
Trade Commission and the National
Labor Relations Board.*

*Congress has created special, as well as
regular, courts:*

*The Claims Court hears claims against
the United States. The Court of International
Trade decides disputes over duties on imported
goods. Their decisions may be appealed to
the Court of Appeals for the Federal Circuit,
which also reviews judgments of the
Patent Office. The Tax Court hears cases of
federal taxation.*

*In the armed services, review normally
ends in the Court of Military Appeals. Beyond
this lies resort to a habeas corpus proceeding
in a district court.*

*Besides cases from federal courts, the
Supreme Court may review decisions of state
judges, when cases involve a federal question
and litigants have no other remedy left.*

Cases from
state courts

U. S. district courts
with federal and local
jurisdiction in the
Virgin Islands, Northern
Mariana Islands, and Guam

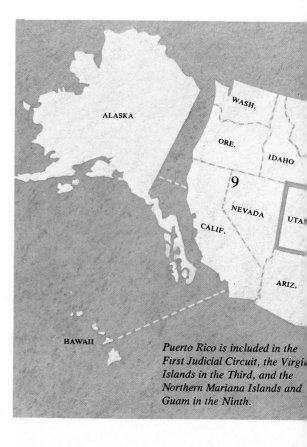

ALASKA

WASH.

ORE.

IDAHO

9

NEVADA

UTA?

CALIF.

ARIZ.

HAWAII

*Puerto Rico is included in the
First Judicial Circuit, the Virgi
Islands in the Third, and the
Northern Mariana Islands and
Guam in the Ninth.*

The Supreme Court of the United States

RICHARD SCHLECHT

U. S. Courts of Appeals

U. S. Court of International Trade

U. S. district courts with federal jurisdiction only in the 50 states, D. C., Puerto Rico, the Virgin Islands, Northern Mariana Islands, and Guam

U. S. executive and administrative agencies

U. S. Claims Court

The Federal Judicial Circuits

THE UNITED STATES *is served by 12 regional federal judicial circuits, ranging in size from the enormous Ninth to the District of Columbia. Each has its own court of appeals and a varying number of district, or trial, courts—94 in all. Circuits also vary in personnel. The First has 4 appellate and 23 district judges; the Ninth, 23 appellate and 73 district judges. Caseloads mount up unevenly, reflecting regional differences in population and social stresses. The Court of Appeals for the Federal Circuit was created in 1982 and serves the entire Nation. It hears appeals from the Claims Court and the Court of International Trade, as well as cases involving special subjects designated by Congress, such as patents.*

"**BOARD OF DIRECTORS**" *of the federal judiciary, members of the Judicial Conference of the United States listen to Chief Justice Rehnquist, their chairman. Created by Congress in 1922 to carry on "a continuous study of . . . the general rules of practices and procedure," the Conference includes the chief judge and a district judge from each of the 12 circuits and the chief judges of the Court of Appeals for the Federal Circuit and the U. S. Court of International Trade. The Conference establishes standards of court policy ranging from the administration of the bankruptcy system to the enforcement of codes of judicial ethics.*

federal courts. These councils thus have obvious value for all concerned.

Although a grievance procedure for federal prisons, introduced in 1973, provides inmates a means of seeking relief from alleged abuses, petitioning the courts continues to be a common recourse. Almost 15,000 grievances are reviewed annually by the Federal Bureau of Prisons; nevertheless, more than 4,500 prisoners still petitioned federal judges

in fiscal 1987. Their complaints receive careful attention. Although some may be trivial, says Senior Judge Walter E. Hoffman, "you can't risk missing a genuine wrong."

Of the three coequal branches of the federal government, the judicial is by far the smallest. Exclusive of the Supreme Court, its employees numbered only 18,277 in 1986; its budget was $1.04 billion, or about one-tenth of one percent of the total federal budget for that year.

"Our work has a devastating finality," comments Senior Judge Ruggero J. Aldisert

of the Third Circuit. "A decision of our court might define the rights of 20 million people for 20 years. But we're out here with the people, all the time. And we're pretty much human beings—even if people think we probably wear black bathrobes at home."

By change and by continuity, the federal court system seeks to guard the rights of every individual. And as the great Chief Justice John Marshall said, this system "comes home in its effects to every man's fireside; it passes on his property, his reputation, his life, his all."

157

Index

Boldface numerals indicate illustrations.

PRINTED BY UNITED COLOR PRESS, INC., MONROE, OHIO

DAVID J. BREWER
1890-1910

HENRY B. BROWN
1891-1906

GEORGE SHIRAS, JR.
1892-1903

HOWELL E. JACKSON
1893-95

WILLIAM RUFUS DAY
1903-22

WILLIAM H. MOODY
1906-10

HORACE H. LURTON
1910-14

CHARLES E. HUGHES*
1910-16; 1930-41

WILLIS VAN DEVANTER
1911-37

WILLIAM H. TAFT*
1921-30

GEORGE SUTHERLAND
1922-38

PIERCE BUTLER
1923-39

EDWARD T. SANFORD
1923-30

STANLEY F. REED
1938-57

FELIX FRANKFURTER
1939-62

WILLIAM O. DOUGLAS
1939-1975

FRANK MURPHY
1940-49

JAMES F. BYRNES
1941-42

SHERMAN MINTON
1949-56

EARL WARREN*
1953-69

JOHN M. HARLAN
1955-71

WILLIAM J. BRENNAN, JR.
1956-

ABE FORTAS
1965-69

THURGOOD MARSHALL
1967-

WARREN E. BURGER*
1969-1986

HARRY A. BLACKMUN
1970-

LEWIS F. POWELL, JR.
1972-1987

EDWARD D. WHITE*
1894-1921

RUFUS W. PECKHAM
1896-1909

JOSEPH McKENNA
1898-1925

OLIVER W. HOLMES
1902-32

JOSEPH R. LAMAR
1911-16

MAHLON PITNEY
1912-22

JAMES C. McREYNOLDS
1914-41

LOUIS D. BRANDEIS
1916-39

JOHN H. CLARKE
1916-22

HARLAN FISKE STONE*
1925-46

OWEN J. ROBERTS
1930-45

BENJAMIN N. CARDOZO
1932-38

HUGO L. BLACK
1937-71

ROBERT H. JACKSON
1941-54

WILEY B. RUTLEDGE
1943-49

HAROLD H. BURTON
1945-58

FRED M. VINSON*
1946-53

TOM C. CLARK
1949-67

CHARLES E. WHITTAKER
1957-62

POTTER STEWART
1958-1981

BYRON R. WHITE
1962-

ARTHUR J. GOLDBERG
1962-65

WILLIAM H. REHNQUIST*
1972-

JOHN PAUL STEVENS
1975-

SANDRA DAY O'CONNOR
1981-

ANTONIN SCALIA
1986-

ANTHONY M. KENNEDY
1988-

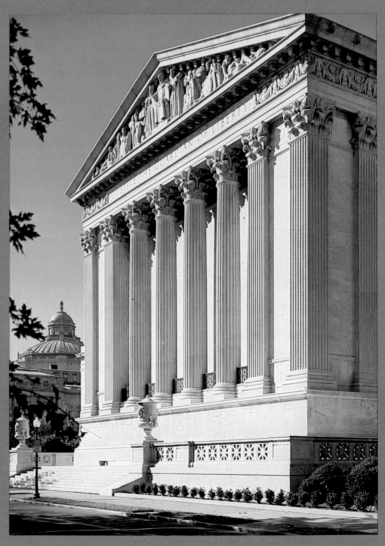

$12.95 (PB)   0-914785-03-6
Equal Justice Under Law
Distributed by
THE SEWALL COMPANY
Box 529   Lincoln, MA 01773